Empath Book

How to Awaken Your Superpower, Protect Yourself Against Emotional Overload, and Live an Empowered Life

Empath Secrets

PUBLISHED BY: Amy White
©Copyright 2021 - All rights reserved.

All rights reserved. No part of this publication may be reproduced, distributed, or transmitted in any form or by any means, including photocopying, recording, or other electronic or mechanical methods, without the prior written permission of the publisher, except in the case of brief quotations embodied in critical reviews and certain other noncommercial uses permitted by copyright law.

Under no circumstances will any blame or legal responsibility be held against the publisher, or author, for any damages, reparation, or monetary loss due to the information contained within this book, either directly or indirectly.

Legal Notice:

This book is copyright protected. It is only for personal use. You cannot amend, distribute, sell, use, quote or paraphrase any part, or the content within this book, without the consent of the author or publisher.

Disclaimer Notice:

Please note the information contained within this document is for educational and entertainment purposes only. All effort has been executed to present accurate, up to date, reliable, complete information. No warranties of any kind are declared or implied. Readers acknowledge that the author is not engaged in the rendering of legal, financial, medical or professional advice. The content within this book has been derived from various sources. Please consult a licensed professional before attempting any techniques outlined in this book.

By reading this document, the reader agrees that under no circumstances is the author responsible for any losses, direct or indirect, that are incurred as a result of the use of the information contained within this document, including, but not limited to, errors, omissions, or inaccuracies.

Table of Contents

Your Free Gift 1

Introduction... 3

Chapter 1: Know Thyself – A Deeper Insight Into Your Empath Gift 8

Chapter 2: The Cursed Gift – Why You Think Your Gift is a Curse.. 29

Chapter 3: Stepping Into Your Blessing – How to Unlock the Power of Your Empath Gift 45

Chapter 4: Physical and Mental Strategies to Protect Your Energy 57

Chapter 5: How to Awaken Your Superpower and Operate in the Fullness of Your Calling 100

Conclusion 155

Thank you! 161

Resources 164

Empath Secrets

Your Free Gift

As a way of saying thanks for your purchase, I want to offer you a free bonus e-Book called *7 Essential Mindfulness Habits* exclusive to the readers of this book.

To get instant access, just go to:

https://theartofmastery.com/mindfulness

Inside the book, you will discover:

- What is mindfulness meditation?
- Why mindfulness is so effective in reducing stress and increasing joy, composure, and serenity
- Various mindfulness techniques that you can do anytime, anywhere
- 7 essential mindfulness habits to implement starting today
- Tips and fun activities to teach your kids to be more mindful

Introduction

"Create boundaries. Honor Your Limits. Say no. Take a break. Let go. Stay grounded. Nurture your body."
~ Alethia Luna

Are you tired of feeling overwhelmed, exhausted, and drained after being around certain people? Are you tired of feeling frustrated because you know you are capable of doing so much good in the world with your empath gift, but you just can't seem to steer it in the right direction? If you have answered yes to any of these questions, this is exactly where you need to be.

The good news is that once you tap into your empath gift, there are no limits; like a true superhero, you will use your superpower to do great exploits. I can say this with confidence because I used to be right where you are today. Let me tell you a bit about myself.

I knew I was different from an early age; I felt things on a deeper level than most people and had many spiritual encounters. As a child, I saw ghosts all the time, the most memorable being my great-grandmother, whom I had never met nor seen pictures of. As I described her in detail to my mother, I remember the color in her face drained as she steadied herself against the desk. Since high sensitivity was not the norm in my family, all my "weird" behaviors were brushed under the carpet, and I was labeled as the "strange one" who no one took seriously. When I would burst into tears while watching what I considered to be a horrific scene on TV, such as a fight or a student being told off by their teacher, my parents would tell me to stop being silly, and my brothers would laugh at me.

As a result, I went through life suppressing my emotions. I never spoke about how I felt in fear of being judged. I jumped from one abusive relationship to the next and ended up marrying one of those abusers. I was tormented in that marriage for almost a decade, and it took every ounce of strength I had to leave. I was completely broken after the divorce. I had hit rock bottom; I was lost and severely depressed. But I had to get better for my two children because I was deteriorating in front of them, and they were absorbing my negative energy.

It was during therapy that I discovered I was an empath; the universe has a funny way of leading you to your destiny. My therapist was an awakened empath who was in full control of her superpower. She became my mentor and taught me everything I know.

Today, I am a proud empath full of power, strength, and vitality. I use my gift to enrich my environment and make the world a better place. What I carry is no longer a burden, but a blessing, and you can experience the same freedom if you desire.

This book is not a quick fix. There is no shortcut to awakening your superpower. It is going to take some serious work on your part. All I can do is provide you with the tools you need to strengthen your gift, but the rest is up to you. Remember, you can have all the knowledge in the world, but if it's not applied, you won't reap the benefits. Here is what you can expect:

- A full understanding of what it means to be an empath
- The common challenges experienced by empaths
- Strategies to protect yourself against emotional overload
- How to embrace and awaken your gift

Life is too short to remain in your current condition. I wish I could give you a magic pill and tell you everything would be okay once you swallow it. But, unfortunately, there is no easy road to destiny. You came into the world for a reason. You have an assignment to complete, and unless you become who you were called to be, you are going to do humanity a huge disservice. Think about it like this: I would never have written this book if my therapist hadn't tapped into her gift and passed the baton on to me. What am I trying to tell you here? That you fulfilling your purpose will determine whether the people you've been assigned to help on Earth fulfill theirs.

I can tell you from my own personal experience that once you start operating in the fullness of your empath gift, a whole new world will open up to you. Depression and sickness will leave you. Narcissists will be afraid of you! Yes... you heard right. Once an empath knows how to control their power, they give off a different type of energy, and you will have a protective shield around you that will only allow them to come so far. As I mentioned, I have been in abusive relationships all my life. All my partners were narcissists, including my ex-husband. But something extraordinary happened when I tapped into my empath gift. Narcissists would sniff around, but they wouldn't stay. First, now that I knew who I was, my discernment was in top shape, and I could spot a narcissist a mile off, so my defenses immediately went up when they approached me. And second, narcissists don't like confident women because they can't manipulate them.

When you learn how to shield yourself, you will be able to connect with people on a deeper level. Once you are fully enlightened, you will radiate power and project your energy in a way that brings healing to others. Think Mother Theresa. She was an empath to the highest degree, and she was a natural caregiver who dispersed love and compassion everywhere she went.

You will learn to harness your creative ability, and whatever path you choose, you will excel in it. Oprah Winfrey and Nicole Kidman are famous empaths who have connected so strongly with their inner genius that they are known across the world for their talent.

You are a part of a unique group of individuals with the power to change, nourish, and heal the world. If you are ready to step into your destiny and wear your superpower with pride, allow me to lead you on the journey of a lifetime as I give you access to the secrets that gave me full control over my empath gift.

Chapter 1: Know Thyself – A Deeper Insight Into Your Empath Gift

"To feel intensely is not a symptom of weakness, it is the trademark of the truly alive and compassionate."
~ Anthon St. Maarten

When a superhero discovers their superpower, the first step is to work out what they can do with it, their limits, and most importantly, how they intend to use it. I totally understand that right now, you don't feel like you've got a superpower. I used to feel like I had a super weakness; but trust me, you are a warrior, and I'm going to teach you exactly how to tap into the deepest crevices of your gift so that you can become the force of nature you were created to be. So, let's start by defining exactly what it means to be an empath.

What is an Empath?

Empathy is a state of being or an emotion that allows people to have an emotional connection with others. It is walking in someone else's shoes so you can see the world from their perspective. The ability to relate to others in this way strengthens personal and professional relationships. It is normal to feel empathy for others; it is a part of what makes us human. However, empaths experience empathy with a huge degree of intensity. Instead of being able to see the world from someone else's perspective, they have the ability to feel exactly what someone else is feeling. Empaths are deeply in tune with the emotions of others, they read facial expressions, and they sense emotions before they've been articulated.

Most people are not familiar with the term *empath*. It's not a psychological disorder, so it doesn't get that kind of attention. But it is a unique personality trait, and experts have started paying attention to it. Here are some scientific explanations for some of the peculiarities associated with being an empath:

Mirroring Emotions: Unless we are fully aware, empaths don't realize that they are mirroring other people's emotions. This unconscious act is why we feel so drained when we've been in the presence of negative people. MRI scans have shown that when highly empathetic individuals pay attention to an emotional person, the same neural circuits are fired off in the brain, and this is what makes the empath feel another's emotions (Lacobani, 2008).

Mirroring Actions: MRI scans indicate that empaths have a neural relay mechanism in the brain, which allows them to imitate the facial expressions, mannerisms, and postures of others. This also applies to minor movements such as someone getting pricked by a needle. If an empath witnesses this, the same sensory and motor areas are activated in the empath's brain, and they react in the same way as the person who was pricked (McLaren, 2013).

Feeling the Pain of Others: A study published in the *Journal of Patient Experience*[1] reported that highly empathetic people felt the electric shock that was administered to a different group. The research involved connecting 16 women to a brain imaging machine and giving them an electric shock. The machine highlighted the areas of the brain that were activated when the women were in pain. The same group of women were then told when their partners, who were in another room, were given an electric shock. The same pain receptors in the women's brains were activated because they were feeling the pain of their partners being given an electric shock.

More Responsive to People in Distress: Are you the type that's always rushing to help someone when they're in distress? Scientists say that's because the brains of people with high empathy are more likely to "code" the correct responses to positive or negative experiences. For example, if your friend was to win the lottery, instead of feeling jealous, your brain has coded the right response so you would be genuinely happy for your friend. If a stranger was in distress, your brain has coded the correct response to their pain, which is to help them.

Signs That You Are an Empath

The reason why scientists started studying empaths is because there are certain behavioral traits that are specific to this personality type. Here are some of them:

You Tune Into the Emotions of Others: This is the foundation of the empath gift—the ability to see the world through the eyes of another. Empaths are so intuitive that they know what someone is trying to say even when they are having difficulty articulating it.

People Always Go to You for Advice: Because of your compassionate nature and your ability to understand where others are coming from, people always go to you for advice, encouragement, and support. Empaths are also very good listeners, and because they are not self-seeking, they would rather listen to someone talk about themselves. And since people like talking about themselves, your good listening skills make you very attractive to those who need to open up about their problems.

You Don't Like Violence: You find it difficult to watch violence on TV or to see it in real life. As mentioned, empaths feel the emotions of others, and sometimes physical pain of others. So when they witness violence, they feel it.

Intimate Relationships Are Challenging: Relationships are always going to have their challenges, but these challenges are magnified for empaths. You sense all your partner's irritations, moods; they can never get away with lying to you because you can tell. You even find positive emotions difficult to handle because they can become overwhelming when you are with your partner all the time. These issues are compounded if you decide to live together because now you are permanently surrounded by someone else's energy. Sometimes you will feel as if your partner is intruding on your space. Empaths love their homes because it is a safe haven for them, somewhere they can disconnect from the rest of the world and bask in their own energy. For this reason, some empaths just don't get involved in relationships while others adapt by having a room in their home where they can have some alone time.

People Feel Safe Around You: As an empath, your energy is attractive, and people are drawn to you. They seek you out because they feel peaceful when they are in your presence. Although this is good for the other person, it is rarely good for you because a person looking for peace typically carries negative energy.

You Are Sensitive to Sensations, Smells, and Sounds: Not only are empaths sensitive to emotions, but they are also sensitive to their environment. Sounds can provoke an emotional response; you prefer to read information instead of listening to it through a media outlet. Some empaths report that they don't like hugging because when they get too close to people, they feel their energy more intensely.

You Feel the Energy in a Room: When I was in my teens, I went clubbing a lot. My friends had a love/hate relationship with me because I would drag them from club to club looking for the right energy. Once I found it, I would have the time of my life. This is a common trait amongst empaths. You can feel the energy of a room as soon as you walk into it. And if it's bad, you will leave.

You Get Overwhelmed in Public: Some empaths find it difficult to go out in public because when there are a lot of people around, and emotions are flying high, the empath catches them, and if they are negative, they get overwhelmed.

More Adventurous: You are more likely to join in and try something you are unfamiliar with if you see someone else having fun. On the other hand, if you observe a person struggling while engaging in the same activity, you are less likely to take part. Again, this is because you sense the positive and negative energy radiating off the individual taking part in the activity.

You Need to Recharge: Tuning in to other people's energy all the time is draining. Therefore, empaths find that they go through periods where they are always tired. When they get to this stage, they've got to take a break from the rest of the world and recharge their batteries. Empaths are often mistaken for introverts because of the amount of time they spend alone. But whether an empath is an introvert or an extrovert, they will get to a point where they need to spend time alone.

Types of Empaths

In the same way there are different superheroes, there are also a variety of empaths. Here are some of the most common types:

Physical Empath: A backache one day, a stomachache the next, depression, panic disorder, and a host of other health conditions that medicine can't seem to resolve. Sound familiar? Physical empaths don't have a protective barrier, and they don't know how to effectively protect themselves. As a result, negative emotional energy manifests into physical pain. In general, empaths tend to be well loved, but people find physical empaths annoying because they are always sick, and no matter how sick they really are, they are often accused of being hypochondriacs. Additionally, doctors can never seem to find anything wrong with them. That's because the emotion is masked as a sickness, and doctors can't diagnose emotions. Here are some signs that you are a physical empath:

- You often feel overwhelmed by the world and have no desire to go outside
- You are always tired and suffer from symptoms that doctors can't explain
- Hostile and angry people make you feel exhausted
- You feel sick, tied, and uneasy in crowds, so you avoid them
- Friends and family label you as too sensitive
- People with bad energy make you want to fall asleep

Emotional Empath: Emotional empaths don't feel things with five fingers; it's like they've got 50 fingers and feel everything ten times more. They literally absorb every emotion they are exposed to. Emotional empaths find it difficult to be in relationships because they get so caught up in the other person that they lose themselves. But at the same time, they get so drained by other people's energy that they need to spend a lot of time alone to process their emotions and recharge.

I am an emotional empath. It's a very challenging gift because, in as much as you desperately want to help people with their problems, you also want to get as far away from them as possible when you start feeling that pull on your energy. I attracted friends who spent the majority of their time complaining and trapped in a never-ending cycle of negativity. My friends assumed I was the happy-go-lucky positive person but what they didn't know was that I was in an abusive relationship, and I suffered from chronic depression. It's an interesting dichotomy because we are so good at hiding our emotions because we don't want to feel like a burden on other people, but at the same time, we really have no idea how we feel because we are so absorbed in other people's emotions.

There were days when I'd just turn off my phone. I couldn't handle the emotional overwhelm that came with an hour-long conversation about all my friend's life problems. To sum it up, emotional empaths are like sponges. They soak up everything around them.

Intuitive Empath: I think the intuitive empath is one of the most powerful because they have the ability to discern between their feelings and the feelings of others. One of the major challenges empaths are faced with is connecting so strongly with other people's feelings that they take ownership of them. The negative energy of others pollutes their inner world. It's easy for them to morph into the people they are surrounded by because they absorb their energy with such intensity. When an empath is in close proximity to an angry person, they get angry. When they are with a sad person, they start feeling sad.

Intuitive empaths don't have this problem. They are so in touch with who they are that they can quickly determine that the emotions they are feeling don't belong to them. The emotions of others don't influence intuitive empaths. Although they deeply empathize with the feelings of others, they are better able to control the barrier that they create between theirs and other people's feelings.

Earth Empath: Do you get a headache when it's about to rain? Or can you sense when a natural disaster is about to take place? If so, you are probably an Earth empath. They have a strong connection to the earth's core. The rush and flow of a waterfall can energize and exhilarate an empath, whereas the toxins in air pollution can make them feel depressed, exhausted, or sick. You feel the earth's changes in your body and draw energy from the sun and the moon. Your body has an intimate connection with the earth, and it sustains and nourishes you. Earth empaths are known to suffer from Seasonal Affective Disorder (SAD)—this is where depression kicks in when the days start getting shorter.

The elements in the universe feel like family to you, the stars and the moon are your companions. When you look up at night, you long to be way up in the heavens dancing with the stars. You'd rather sit out under the moonlit sky than have a night out with friends. Earth empaths feel the love of the earth. You hate the way people treat nature when they cut trees down and pour oil in the sea, and you are deeply hurt by the destruction of the planet in this way. When the earth is in pain, it groans; you can hear it and connect with it.

Earth empaths are also known to have premonitions about natural disasters. You enjoy connecting with the earth by walking barefoot on the grass and swimming in the lakes, rivers, or ocean. Earth empaths tune into the earth's vibrations by asking how it feels and waiting for any intuitions they can tap into.

Animal Empath: I'm a bit of a history buff, and I seem to always spot the old-time empaths, and one famous animal empath was Saint Francis of Assisi. He had a deep love for animals and was known for his ability to communicate with them in a unique way. During medieval times, you were not seen in a favorable light if you had a connection with animals and nature. This was especially true if a person held views about animals or nature that didn't line up with church doctrine. It was not uncommon for animal lovers to be accused of witchcraft or demonic possession. Gosh! It infuriates me when I think of that, how terrible it must have been not to be able to express your love for those precious creatures.

But Saint Francis of Assisi got a pass because his unique ability was seen as a sign of holiness and not something evil. One of his most well-known feats was when he tamed the wolf of Gubbio. What he achieved was labeled as a miracle, but I just think he was an animal empath. Certain aspects of his life point to this, especially the fact that he lived in isolation. He didn't like being around people and spent long periods of his life alone. People thought he was alone, but I suspect he was basking in the comfort of wild animals, and it was during these times that he developed his superpowers. Hence his ability to tame the wolf. Food for thought, right?

Anyway, animal empaths recognize the mental state and emotions of animals. The interesting thing is that all animals express themselves differently. It is believed that insects don't have emotions, so we will leave them out of the equation. But a dog doesn't express itself in the same way as an elephant does. A dog expresses their love, happiness, and excitement by jumping to get on the same level as the person they are excited about. An elephant, on the other hand, express their excitement by blaring and bellowing. This is typically done when they get together with friends and family in the wild.

At the Matobo Hills National Park in Zimbabwe, there is a popular scout affectionately nicknamed "Lizardman" who communicates with small lizards and has done so for many years. His father taught him this skill, and he is able to touch and feed them from his hand. He is the only person capable of doing this; the lizards won't go to anyone else but him regardless of the food they try to offer them. The lizards only trust the scout because he is an animal empath and connects with them on a spiritual level.

Animal empaths often become animal behaviorists or ethologists. Another well-known animal empath is lion expert Kevin Richardson (aka the lion whisperer). He works with spotted hyenas, black leopards, and African lions. He is known to have lived with, fed, and slept with lions.

As mentioned, animal empaths connect with their emotions, and it is not uncommon for them to be vegetarian or vegan because of this. Some empaths have stated that meat tastes like the pain and fear the animal experienced when they were being tortured. But not everyone understands this. One woman describes how she fell out with her boyfriend because of it. She went to visit him in Puerto Rico and found it very distressing to witness such a large population of homeless and starving dogs. During a visit to one of her boyfriend's relatives, they made goat stew for dinner. She was unable to eat the food because she could feel the pain of the animal. Additionally, they told her that it was fresh meat because they had raised the goat themselves and just killed it. To the average person, this would be a dream come true to know exactly where the meat came from. But to her, it was repulsive. There were homeless dogs behind the house, and she managed to sneak out and give the goat stew to the dogs. But her boyfriend caught her and was extremely offended that she was giving food cooked for humans to dogs. She felt ashamed and embarrassed that she felt so deeply for these dogs, and for the rest of her time, she was forced to repress her feelings in fear of being ridiculed again.

Plant Empath: Do you love plants, trees, and everything green? If so, you are probably a plant empath. You have a deep connection with their needs; plants start to wither on the inside before it shows on the outside. Empaths can sense when a plant is in need before its leaves start turning brown because they connect with its spirit. Plant empaths communicate with plants. They have conversations, and the plant will tell the empath what it needs.

Additionally, plant empaths have an attraction to mountains, woods, waterfalls, rivers, and seas. When they are out in nature, they feel as if they are at one with it. Plant empaths often have plants and trees as friends and companions as children. When you got upset (particularly because people didn't understand you), did you run outside and confide in your favorite tree? Going out into nature comforts plant empaths when they are in distress. They like climbing trees, touching, and hugging them.

Empath Secrets

Plant empaths bring the best out in plants because of their ability to tune in to their spirit flowers, and plants draw positive energy from them. Plants respond to the presence and touch of empaths, which is why plant empaths often become gardeners, or get into careers such as landscaping, floral arranging, garden design, botany, and horticulture. Plant empaths function at their best when they are connected to nature.

You will find that a lot of Chinese medicinal herbalists and practitioners are plant empaths. They strongly believe that plants have healing power, and much of their knowledge has been passed down from generations. Many years ago, people were at one with nature. They honored plants and regarded them as intelligent and aware. In those days, tribal shamans would carry messages between the plant and the spirit world. Plants sing and create music; it is this healing power that herbalists tap into to gain access to plant medicine.

Psychometric Empath: This type of empath is capable of receiving memories, energy, and other information from physical objects such as photographs, clothing, and jewelry. They can also connect certain events or situations with and form impressions with physical objects. Basically, psychometric empaths can use and absorb the energy from a certain physical object or place to gather useful information.

For example, someone without this gift will see a ring and think nothing of it. But the psychometric empath sees more than a ring because they connect with the energy that is attached to it. For example, if it's a wedding ring, the psychometric empath will be able to determine whether the marriage is in a good or bad place. They can also sense the age and origin of objects.

Additionally, when a psychometric empath comes into contact with an object connected to trauma, they feel confused and overwhelmed.

Am I an Empath?

There is a chance that you are not an empath but instead a highly sensitive person (HSP). This book isn't about HSPs, so I won't go into detail about this personality trait, but research suggests that 15–20 percent of the population fall into this category. Basically, if you answer no to all of the questions below, you are probably an HSP. Since being an empath is not a psychological disorder, but a personality trait, you can't get a diagnosis for it, but what you can do is self-diagnose. Dr. Judith Orloff is a world-renowned psychologist who has a profound understanding of the empath gift. In her book *The Empath's Survival Guide,* she provides a very helpful survey to determine whether you are indeed an empath. Spend some time answering the following questions:

- Do strong smells, loud talking, and loud noise send me into an emotional meltdown?
- Do I feel emotionally drained when I'm in a crowd of people and need to spend time alone to recover?
- Do I get offended easily?
- If I am around someone who is upset, do I feel their pain?
- Do people think I'm "too sensitive" or "too emotional"?
- Do I prefer to go to social gatherings in my own car, so I am not dependent on anyone when I want to leave?
- Am I afraid to get too deeply involved in an intimate relationship?
- Do I deal with stress by going on food binges?

Now add up your answers. How many did you answer yes to, and how many did you answer no to? Dr. Orloff suggests you are partially empath if yes was your response to one to three questions, and if you answered yes to three or more questions, you are a full-blown empath.

Now that you know what your superpower is, the next step is to understand your limitations. Despite the intensity of our power, every superhero is limited in some way. For example, Cyclops has several restrictions on his powers. One of them is because he was in a car accident that killed his parents. He suffered a head injury, and as a result, he can't turn off his optic blasts. Likewise, as an empath, there are a number of things that will prevent you from operating in the fullness of your gift. We will take a further look at them in the next chapter.

Takeaways

- An empath is someone who is uniquely sensitive to the needs of others. They can feel people's pain because they absorb energy. There are several scientific studies that give us more insight into the psychological aspects of the empath gift. In other words, your gift is not a

- figment of your imagination. You were born this way.
- There are different types of empaths: physical empath, emotional empath, intuitive empath, Earth empath, animal empath, plant empath, and the psychometric empath.
- According to Dr. Judith Orloff, you can self-diagnose as an empath by taking a survey. You will answer questions such as: Do strong smells, loud talking, and loud noise send you into a meltdown? Do you get offended easily? Do you deal with stress by going on food binges?

Chapter 2: The Cursed Gift – Why You Think Your Gift is a Curse

"Speaking the truth is often a struggle for an empath. The last thing they want to do is cause pain or conflict for others." ~ Judy Eisner

Trust me when I say that your empath gift is the most powerful and precious blessing you could have been given. I know how it feels to lie in bed every night and just wish you were "normal." I know what it feels like to wish you could just switch off and stop absorbing everyone's energy. I know what it feels like to hate the fact that you know for a fact that some of your friends are not really for you because you can feel it in their energy. And the list goes on. There are endless reasons why you feel stuck right now. But I promise you that once you learn how to channel your gift in the right direction, you will realize how incredibly blessed you truly are. The good news is that you are not alone in believing your gift is a curse because all superheroes go through this.

When Metamorpho was first ordained with his tremendous powers, he hated his new body. He felt trapped in a form he didn't recognize. Despite the fact that he now had the supernatural ability to transmute the elements he had within him and to shapeshift, his greatest desire was to become human again. His body is now an assortment of bright and vibrant colors, and he is made up of a variety of elements and materials. Metamorpho hates his transformation; as far as he's concerned, it's a curse. When he looks in the mirror, he sees a monster and blames everyone for his misfortune. He refuses to acknowledge the uniqueness of his gift. In particular, that he is the only superhero in the DC Universe that has been given power over death. Unlike other superheroes who have been resurrected, he does it repeatedly. Metamorpho has been killed several times by different enemies, but he keeps coming back to life.

Through Metamorpho, we learn that some superheroes really do despise their gift, and one of the reasons is that it removes them from humanity. However, the message I want to get across is that we all possess the power of choice, and how you choose to view your empath gift is determined by your perspective. Metamorpho refused to see his gift as a blessing. As far as he was concerned, he was suffering from an incurable disease. The consequence of his thought process was that every heroic act was tainted because of the way he thought about his powers. He looked in the mirror and chose to see himself as a monster not worthy of the object of his affection's love. He chose not to find contentment in his life as a superhero. Metamorpho never found rest from his torment because he chose not to.

What am I trying to tell you here? Don't make the same mistake. I can give you a bag full of tools to assist you in beautifying your empath gift, but if you choose to remain a people-pleaser, remain depressed, remain powerless, and continue believing that you are a freak of nature, that's exactly what you are going to get. Remember, James Allen wrote an entire book on the power of our thoughts entitled, *As a Man Thinketh, So Is He*. I am a firm believer that before you can free yourself from something, you've got to acknowledge the problem and understand why it's there. So, here are some of the reasons why you feel your empath gift is a curse.

People-Pleasing Drains You

Empaths are relentless people-pleasers. On the surface, wanting to please people doesn't sound like a bad idea. After all, it's better than making them feel miserable, right? But there is a lot more to people-pleasing than meets the eye. According to therapist Erika Myers, people-pleasing involves compromising your beliefs and values so that you don't cause offense. It involves neglecting yourself so that friends and family members are happy, and this is how people-pleasing becomes an issue. If you are not sure whether you are a people pleaser, here are a few signs:

- **You Want Approval:** People pleasing is one of the many ways that low self-esteem manifests. Because you seek validation from others, you fear that the validation will be withdrawn if you don't give them what they want. In other words, you believe that love is conditional.
- **You Are Afraid of Rejection:** People-pleasers have a deep fear of being rejected. They want people to need them because if someone needs them, they are not going to leave. But once the people you are trying to please reject you, they will no longer need you. Fear is a great motivator to get you to do things you don't want to do.
- **You Are Incapable of Saying No:** The word no is a nonexistent word in the vernacular of a people-pleaser. They say yes to everything

because they don't want to upset anyone. It is their way of keeping the peace, although deep down you don't have peace about the situation because you know it is going to be a great inconvenience to you. Additionally, the inability to say no gives people permission to take advantage of you. This is one of the many reasons why empaths end up stuck in abusive relationships with narcissists.

- **You Take the Blame for Everything:** Empaths don't like confrontation, so if someone accuses you of something, you are just going to accept full responsibility for the transgression despite the fact that you had nothing to do with it. For example, let's say you are told to go and get lunch for your co-workers. Four of them are vegan and ask you to buy them a vegan pizza. You give the customer service assistant the order, and she punches it in correctly because it's written on the receipt. However, the cooks in the kitchen mix your order up, and you end up with the wrong food, but you don't find out until you get to the office. The vegans open their pizzas, which are covered in pepperoni! Your co-workers accuse you of not paying attention to detail and ridicule you for not checking the order before leaving the store. Instead of being assertive and explaining that you gave the right order, and you can back up what you are saying because you have the receipt, you accept full responsibility and apologize for not paying attention to detail. You now think that your co-workers hate you and that they've lost faith in your ability to go out and get lunch for the team.

- **You Are Always Giving:** Your friend walks up to you in the canteen and says, "Hey, can I borrow ten bucks?" Your immediate response is, "Sure." You have just agreed to give your friend your last ten dollars despite the fact that you need it for gas money, and you are not getting paid until the following Friday! Giving is a beautiful thing to do, but sacrificial giving, because you don't want your friend to ditch you, is not healthy.

- **You Are Always Busy:** And you're not busy because you are working on your goals and ambitions, you are busy because all your time is spent doing things for other people.

You Have Depressive Episodes

Let me start by saying that there are levels of depression, and in this section, I am not talking about clinical depression. If you believe you are clinically depressed, it's essential that you get professional help. You will know if you need to see a therapist because you will feel sad all the time, and there is no relief from your turmoil. On the other hand, empaths typically suffer from depressive episodes. A depressive[2] episode lasts for approximately two weeks. During this time, you experience symptoms of depression such as:

- Unexplainable pains in your body
- Thoughts of death and suicide
- Talking or moving slower than normal
- Changes in sleep patterns
- Trouble remembering or concentrating
- A loss of interest in social activities and hobbies
- Changes in appetite and weight
- Restlessness
- Low energy or fatigue
- Frustration or irritability
- Anxiety
- Feeling worthless or guilty

- Feeling helpless, hopeless, or sad

There are several reasons why empaths are more prone to depression. Here are some of them:

- **You Feel Lonely:** Empaths feel lonely because no one understands them. It's not like you've got a crew of empath friends, and you can sit down over coffee and talk about how much energy you've absorbed today! We are rare people, and for that reason, you are going to feel alone sometimes. You have a desperate need to fit in, to stop wearing a mask and wear your gift with pride, but society won't let you. We like watching people with supernatural powers on TV, but to have them walking among us is a different story.
- **Your Nervous System is Being Overworked:** When your nervous system is being hammered because you are dealing with sensory overload, the only way to overcome it is by withdrawing. When you withdraw, people get upset because they don't understand why you don't want to be around them. When they get upset, you get upset, and hence the vicious cycle begins. When empaths are in isolation, instead

of spending that time implementing grounding techniques and recharging their batteries, they get depressed because their focus is on being concerned about what other people think about them because they are self-isolating.

- **Compassion Overload:** Feeling that you've got to take care of everyone's needs is exhausting. You are the one everyone comes to when they need to offload their problems, and you gladly accept because you feel compassion towards them and want to help. The problem is that not only do you take on other people's issues as your own, but you also do it too much. In one day, you might see three friends all for the purpose of you being a shoulder to cry on. As much as you want to help, it makes you feel overwhelmed, and then you end up depressed.

- **You Feel Frustrated:** Empaths internalize their frustration; for example, you know saying yes to driving Aunty Sheila to the airport will mean you will only get two hours sleep. Once you've dropped her off, and you are on your way back, you spend the journey angry because you know you are going to be exhausted at work the next day, and you've got a deadline for a project.

You Feel Powerless

Some empaths feel immobilized by the world because you are in such conflict with it. On the one hand, you want to save the world because there are so many hurting people. On the other hand, you want to disconnect from the world because you hate the fact that it's so cruel. When you feel that you can't move forward in your gift, you become stagnated, and you relinquish your power.

Instead of empaths using their sensitive nature to connect with the powers of healing and restoration that lies deep within them, they give in to the fears that are immobilizing them. Like Metamorpho, you have convinced yourself that the world is a wicked and evil place that has hijacked your ability to operate in the fullness of your gift. In other words, you see yourself as a victim, and you have chosen to see the world through the lens of a victim. You have chosen to withdraw your gift and live from a place of defeat instead of victory.

You Attract Toxic People

And I'm not just talking about narcissists here. I am talking about toxic people in general. Here are some reasons why you attract toxic people:

You Are Honest: Toxic people enjoy tearing people down; it's how they make themselves feel better. In psychology, this is referred to as social undermining[3]; it involves directing your negative emotions towards a person to stop them from achieving their goals. They will criticize your every move, and nothing you do is ever good enough. However, it's harder to criticize someone when you don't have any information about them, and this is where honesty becomes a problem. People who erect boundaries in their lives know not to tell everybody everything. They spot toxic people a mile off and keep them at arm's length. Empaths who are not in full control of their gift don't know how to do this, and they let everyone into their space, even the people who don't deserve to be there. They then overshare with these toxic people, which gives them the ammunition they need to shoot them down.

You Listen: Everyone likes talking about themselves. To a certain extent, there is nothing wrong with this. Sharing information about our personal lives is how we build trust in a relationship because that's how we get to know people. But with toxic people, they are totally uninterested in what's going on in the listener's life.

Even if they ask questions to make it look like they are listening, their response is irrelevant because the conversation will quickly revert back to them. Empaths are good listeners because they are compassionate and can feel your pain, so they want to understand where you are coming from. This is how empaths end up getting trapped in relationships with toxic people. The toxic person is attracted to that listening ear because they know they are not going to have to fight to keep the conversation about them.

You Are Non-Confrontational: There is absolutely nothing wrong with being non-confrontational. You value your peace, and you would like to keep it that way. The problem isn't that you are non-confrontational, the issue is why? Empaths don't like confrontation for several reasons, and the most important is that you have a deep fear of upsetting people because you desperately want them to like you. Instead, when someone offends you, you internalize everything and go into self-destruct mode. Toxic individuals love non-confrontational people because it means their behavior is never challenged. Toxic people refuse to accept responsibility for their actions. When something goes wrong in their lives, they will point the finger at everyone else but themselves. They hate personal reflection because they are forced to look at who they really are, and that is not a pretty picture. When toxic people are around non-confrontationalists, they know they can have full control of their environment. As draining as toxic people are, they feel that being around people who pull them up on their stuff is draining because they are then forced to justify their actions. In a nutshell, empaths make toxic people feel very comfortable.

You Are a Giver: In this instance, I am not talking about acts of giving, such as lending people money. Empaths are givers of themselves. They give away their time, energy, and emotions to the wrong people, and toxic people thrive off this. As mentioned, toxic people are draining. Whatever power you display, they take it. You can't celebrate your wins around a toxic person because they won't congratulate you. Instead, they will find every possible reason to discredit your success. Since you don't like confrontation, you will just accept what the toxic person has to say and accept defeat by playing right into the hand they've just dealt you.

Empath Secrets

You Are a Light: As the saying goes, "opposites attract." Negative people are full of darkness, and they are always looking for some light in their lives, and they will go to extreme lengths to get it. On the flip side of things, empaths feel responsible for everyone's feelings; they think they need to fix everyone. Therefore, they will allow people to violate their boundaries because they think they have to in order to make that person feel whole again.

This chapter could be a book in itself because I've only just scratched the surface about how difficult it is to live as an empath when you don't understand your gift. So many things keep coming at you that you feel as if your world is spinning out of control and you don't have the power to stop it. You are not alone. Many empaths go through this stage, and personally, I believe it's necessary to fully understand how blessed you really are. Victory is always sweeter when you have come from a dark place. I want to end this chapter with a word of encouragement and hope: After your dark nights, you will experience joy in the morning. Your situation is not permanent. This is the road you need to travel to get to your purpose. I am grateful for those dark nights, those times of misery and despair when I felt as if I was behind a locked door trapped in a torture chamber with no escape. The main reason why I am grateful for those times of hopelessness is that I can now fulfill my highest calling because I found the key to get out, and now I can pass it on to others. Empaths have a deep desire to heal the world. You will never tap into the fullness of your healing potential if you can't give people a cure that is guaranteed to work. When your life is the evidence that the antidote works, when it is presented to others with the same problem, they are more willing to accept it. So in the next few chapters, I am going to teach you how to reverse the curse and unleash the blessing of the empath gift.

Takeaways

- You are not alone in believing your superpower is a curse. The superhero Metamorpho hated his gift because he focused on all the things that were wrong with it instead of on the tremendous power that had been made available to him.
- There are several reasons why you feel that your empath gift is a curse. These include: people-pleasing drains you, you have depressive episodes, you feel powerless, you attract toxic people, your non-confrontational nature attracts people who take advantage of you, you

give too much of yourself away to people who don't deserve you, and your light attracts darkness.

Chapter 3: Stepping Into Your Blessing – How to Unlock the Power of Your Empath Gift

"Empaths did not come into this world to be victims; we came to be warriors. Be brave. Stay strong. We need all hands on deck." ~ Anthon St. Maarten

In life, you reap what you sow. My question to you is, are you prepared to do what it takes to activate the blessing that you already possess? In every area of life, training is necessary to become an expert. Most people are born with a natural ability to do something with excellence. They might have the ability to write or play music. Maybe they can sing, write, or dance. But unless these gifts are fine-tuned, their full expression is never revealed. I will use the football star Cristiano Ronaldo as an example. He has a natural ability to play football. He realized he was good at it at the age of eight and spent many years training to perfect his gift. It wasn't until 2003 (ten years after he started playing), that he hit the world stage and joined the premier league team Manchester United. Today, Ronaldo is one of the most talented footballers in the world. Why? Because he spent ten years practicing; the majority of people never get to bless the world with their gift because they don't invest in it. Likewise, you were born with your empath gift, but if you don't nurture it, you won't know how to use it properly. The same is true of superheroes. They've got to practice their gift before it becomes a superpower. Let me tell you why.

Your Habits Will Determine Your Outcome

One of my favorite films is *The Karate Kid*. I used to watch it every Sunday morning with my sisters during my childhood years. Daniel Larusso is the main character in the film. He had just moved to a new town, and he was getting bullied. One day, during an attack, a karate expert came out of nowhere and saved Daniel. This man was named Mr. Miyagi, and he managed to fight off a gang of attackers who were half his age. Daniel Larusso was so impressed with the incredible skills Mr. Miyagi possessed that he asked him to train him in karate so that he could protect himself. Mr. Miyagi reluctantly agreed, and his training commenced. Mr. Miyagi was the expert. He knew what Daniel needed to do to get to his level, but Daniel wasn't impressed with what he was being taught.

On the first day of training, Mr. Miaygi had Daniel waxing cars. The next day he was told to sand wooden floors. On day three, he paints the fences in Mr. Miyagi's garden using vertical strokes. The next day, Daniel is told to paint Mr. Miyagis's house using horizontal strokes. The next day he is told to start working on another chore, but by this time, Daniel is completely fed up because he believes that Mr. Miyagi is not teaching him karate but using him for free labor to get his house in order. As Daniel goes to walk out of the door, Mr. Miyagi stops him and tells him to wax the car, sand the floor, paint the fence, and paint the house. Mr. Miyagi throws a punch with each move, and Daniel is able to block every one of them without even thinking about it.

Why am I telling you about *The Karate Kid*? Because there is an important lesson I want you to learn. When I watched the film as a child, I believed that Mr. Miyagi was training Daniel in that way so he would become familiar with the moves required to learn karate. Strangely enough, it was my therapist who told me to watch the film, not knowing that it was my all-time favorite movie. After I watched the film, we had another session, and she started teaching me about muscle memory. Stay with me, please; I'm going somewhere with this.

The Power of Muscle Memory

Mr. Miyagi was getting Daniel to repeat those actions so that they would become a memory in his brain, and when necessary, the brain would send a signal to the muscles to make the required movement needed to carry out the skill. So when Daniel was able to block the punches and kicks that Mr. Miyagi was launching at him, he did it automatically because he had spent so much time practicing it. Even though Daniel wasn't born with the gift of karate, he practiced it so much until it became a superpower, and he eventually won the tournament against the same people who had defeated him at the start of the film. Every martial arts expert understands that martial arts are about training habits and responses until they become natural, and this is done through repetition.

Your empath gift does not involve physical movements, but in order to become an expert at anything, you've got to practice, and that process takes place and is solidified in the brain, and this is where muscle memory comes into the equation. When empaths don't understand their gift, they adopt certain habits to shield themselves. Everything you read in Chapter Two is about the habits empaths develop that lead them to believe their blessing is a curse. In order to step into the blessing of your gift, you've got to unlearn all those negative habits and adopt the habits that will unlock your full potential as an empath. In other words, you've got to unlearn muscle memory. Your brain has been trained to get depressed, accept toxic people, people please, and everything else that comes with the accursed status of the empath gift.

You have become stuck in this habit loop not because you are weak, but because you didn't know any better. If someone had trained you from childhood how to use your empath gift as a superpower, you would be a real-life superhero right now. You are suffering on a subconscious level, and you will find the solution through the application of three steps:

1. Awareness
2. Commitment
3. Retraining

Awareness – Shining the Light on Your Bad Habits

Let me start by asking you a question. Do you want to unlearn the negative habits you've learned surrounding your empath gift? I am assuming you've said yes. Great! We can move forward now.

What is the Habit? The first step to changing a bad habit is to become aware of it. So to begin, I want you to sit down, get a pen and paper, and write out all the reasons why you think your empath gift is a curse. Now go through the list and write a detailed description of each one of those "curses." For example, if you have written about the habit of depressive episodes, don't just focus on how it makes you feel; describe how it impacts different areas of your life. Do you call in sick for work, turn your phone off and miss important announcements from friends and family members, etc.? Describing the habit is an important step in the process because before you can eliminate a bad habit, you need to have a full understanding of why you want to change it. You can then use this information to motivate yourself when you want to give up, because trust me, those times are going to come.

Educate Yourself: One of the main reasons why people fail to break out of bad habits is because they don't understand how detrimental it is to their overall well-being. Now it's time to do some research, learn everything you can about the specifics of each negative habit, and write down what you are learning.

Monitor the Habit: Now that you have a better understanding of the bad habit, start monitoring and recording the habit. It is advised that you spend up to two weeks monitoring these habits. Pay attention to the following:

- How often does the habit take place?
- Is there a certain time that it happens?
- What is the mental and physical process before you engage in the habit?
- Is there anyone else there when it happens?

Evaluate Your Findings: The next step is to spend time evaluating your findings. Pay attention to the following:

- What is the specific impact it is having on your life? Are your productivity levels dropping? Does it make you late for work?
- What are the circumstances that are leading you to this habit?

Commitment to Your Freedom

No one is going to come and rescue you from your prison. Life doesn't work like that. There are no handouts. There is no personal trainer who's going to wake you up every morning and sit there with you while you engage your brain. Whether you succeed or fail in life is dependent upon the effort you put into arriving at your final destination. I once saw a photo of bloody ballerina feet. I don't know what anyone else took from the photo, but I was reminded that watching a ballerina glide so effortlessly across a stage takes commitment and dedication. The blood on her feet was symbolic of how hard she worked to acquire her position. When it looks like people are operating in excellence with little to no effort, we have no idea how many hours of practice went into perfecting that skill.

I can totally relate to this; I have several empath mentees who are in awe of my gift, and they can't wait until they reach my level. I tell them all the time that I didn't just arrive here. It has taken years of practice. From the outside looking in, it looks like I'm just flowing in my gift, but the only reason why I can flow in it is because I've mastered the art of flowing in it.

One of the main reasons why people love watching sports is not just because they enjoy the game. It's a chance to admire those who have invested in themselves so much that they became an expert sportsman or woman. The reality is that most people don't want extraordinary results without doing what is required to achieve those results. A-grade students are naturally intelligent, but they have also spent time studying their subject so that they know the answers to the questions when they are presented. They are often called names like "teacher's pet" and "Boffin" because their teachers praise them for their strong work ethic. But the people doing the name-calling are sitting in front of the TV every night instead of studying. The bottom line is that your commitment will determine your outcome. Don't be an empath who never walks in the fullness of their calling because they didn't have enough willpower to commit.

Retraining

Bad habits are not eliminated; they are replaced. As you have read, the bad habits that have led you to believe that your empath gift is a curse have been developed over time. Despite the fact that they are self-destructive, they are a benefit to you in some way. I used to have a

Empath Secrets

bad habit of binge eating in response to overwhelm; as a result, I ended up severely overweight. The benefit for me was that I had convinced myself that if I get fat, I will be able to protect myself from the negative energy that keeps on attaching itself to me. But I would only get like this when I felt overwhelmed. I would lock myself in the house and buy loads of takeaway and sweet treats. Once I had got over the overwhelm, I felt disgusted with myself, and vowed never to do it again. But as the story goes, the vicious cycle continued.

So, how do you retrain yourself and get rid of these bad habits? Good question. Here are the steps you will need to implement:

Replacement: On a piece of paper, draw a line down the middle. On one side, write *bad habits*, and on the other side, write *good habits*. Start by writing down all the bad habits you want to change, and then write down the good habits you want to replace them with. For example, as mentioned, I used to binge eat when I got overwhelmed. I swapped the bad habit of binge eating for the good habit of meditation.

Support: You are going to need all the support you can get because this is not an easy task. Confide in someone you trust and let them know your plans. It would be great if you had another empath friend to work with. But if not, that's fine. Just get some support.

Positive People: As you know, empaths have a tendency to attract negative people because of the light that's in them. I am not expecting you to start blocking everyone you know who gives off negative energy but keep them at arm's length as much as possible. When you do decide to be around people, make sure they are upbeat and positive because the less depressed you feel, the less likely you are going to engage in bad habits.

Visualization: Empaths have got wild imaginations, so you will be good at this. Spend time visualizing your success. I got into a habit of doing this twice a day, and it worked like a charm for me.

- Sit or lie in a comfortable position and take a few deep breaths.
- Imagine you are in a really nice location like a beach or a park. Think about what you can see, hear, smell, touch, and taste. Engage with every emotion that comes with what you are visualizing

- Imagine yourself happy, healthy, and free from every bad habit that is holding you captive.
- Do this exercise for ten minutes twice a day.

You are not going to ditch your bad habits overnight. It is going to take a conscious, determined effort to push yourself through this. The good news is that I know it's possible if you refuse to give up and keep trying.

Takeaways

- Your habits will determine your outcome. What you repeatedly do is who you will become. If you want to live in the fullness of your superpower, you've got to break all bad habits.
- You developed bad habits because they are ingrained in your muscle memory. But you can change your muscle memory in three steps: becoming aware of your bad habits and how they are affecting your life, committing to changing those bad habits, and retraining yourself by replacing the bad habits with good habits.

Chapter 4: Physical and Mental Strategies to Protect Your Energy

"Being an empath is a huge asset when you learn to manage it." ~ Judith Orloff

All superheroes have a secret identity. When Spiderman isn't trapping criminals, he is Peter Parker. When Batman isn't playing the hero on the streets of Gotham, he is Bruce Wayne. And when Superman isn't saving the day in his blue and red outfit, he's the shy, well-mannered news reporter Clark Kent. Why do superheroes conceal their identity? Could you imagine if they didn't? Their phones would never stop ringing, and their doors would never stop knocking. The superheroes' secret identity is the way they protect their energy; they can step in and out of their role when they feel like it. I bet you're thinking, *I wish I could do that.* Well, I'm here to tell you that you can, and here's how.

Set Boundaries at Work and at Home

The easiest strategy to implement is to set boundaries. Even though it's the easiest, let me warn you, it's not

Empath Secrets

easy! Especially because we are empaths and we find it difficult to be assertive, but the more you enforce these boundaries, the easier it will become. Let's start by defining the term boundaries.

What Are Boundaries?

In a nutshell, boundaries are imaginary fences you place around yourself that tells others how far they can go. According to marriage and family therapist Jenn Kennedy[4], boundaries provide protection for our physical and emotional space. Think about it like this. When there is a fence around a garden, a normal person isn't going to climb over the fence and walk on the lawn. If they need anything, they are going to find a way to get that person's attention and ask. Boundaries act in the same way. When those around you know you've set them, they are not going to walk into your space without you inviting them in.

When you don't set boundaries, it has a negative effect on your mental health. This is one of the main reasons why you always feel drained. Not only are these people sucking your energy dry, but having your space constantly violated is also psychologically damaging.

Mental health counselor Justin Baksh states that your identity and self-esteem will take a bashing when you keep honoring intrusions in your life. Deep down, you resent the people who keep bothering you, but you are too afraid to tell them to stop.

How to Set Boundaries

Your first step is to determine who is violating your personal and emotional space. Sit down with a pen and a notepad and draw a line down the middle of a sheet of paper. On one side, write the name of the person, and on the other side, write down how they intrude on your space. For example, your best friend might have a habit of calling you in the middle of the night to talk about the argument they've just had with their partner. These frequent late-night phone calls are frustrating to you because it's important to have uninterrupted sleep throughout the night, but sleep is even more important for empaths because that's one of the ways we charge our energy.

You might be in an intense relationship where your partner expects to see you every day. After work, they just turn up at your house and plonk themselves on the couch.

At work, your manager might come to your desk several times a day, giving you tasks that are not a part of your job description. Basically, they are palming off their work to you because they know you will do it without question. Or, maybe you get attacked by the resident gossipmonger on your lunch breaks. As soon as you sit down to eat, here she comes chewing your ear off about what happened when the team went out for drinks last night.

When it comes to setting boundaries, don't pick up the phone and call everyone on your list and tell them about your new rules. Wait until the violation occurs and then say something. Otherwise, you will come off as confrontational and probably offend the person. With the friend who calls in the middle of the night, the next time she does, answer the phone and say, "I'm really tired right now. I would be grateful if you could call me tomorrow when I'm well rested and in a better frame of mind to talk. With that being said, I would really appreciate it if you could stop calling me in the middle of the night after an argument with your partner. I've noticed that I find it difficult to concentrate at work when you call so late." This news will shock your friend, as they are not used to you putting up any resistance towards their demands. But don't engage in an argument with them. There is no need to explain yourself any further than you already have. Wish the person a good night and hang up.

Now, boundaries should always come with consequences. However, there is no need to mention them the first time around. Most people will get the message and give you the space you are asking for. But if they violate the boundary you've set, that is when you mention the consequences. So a week later, your friend calls back at 1 a.m. As soon as you answer the phone, get straight to the point, and say, "Didn't I ask you not to call me at this time of the night?" People who have no respect for boundaries will have every excuse under the sun as to why they've got the right to break them. Don't even listen to an explanation; shut it down immediately by saying, "Listen, if this happens again, I will put my phone on *do not disturb* during the night so that you can't get through." If it happens again, don't even answer the phone. Hit the *reject* button, change the settings on your phone, and go back to sleep. It is essential that you enforce the consequences. If not, the boundary breaker won't take you seriously, and they will keep violating your space.

How about when your partner keeps turning up at your house every evening? The next time they turn up, politely tell them how much you love their company, and you really value spending time with them, but you need a couple of days a week to yourself. Again, this will probably shock your partner. They may even get a little upset and assume you don't want to be with them anymore. Reassure your partner that you don't want to break up, you just need space to be by yourself sometimes. You don't need to give a lengthy explanation, just leave it at that. Once you both agree on your alone days and your partner turns up anyway, tell them about the consequences. You could say something like, "I have told you I need to be alone a couple of times a week. We agreed that the days were Tuesday and Thursday, but it seems you've ignored my requests." Don't give them a chance to explain. Just say, "The next time it happens, you would have wasted your time driving all the way down here because I won't answer the door." If your partner returns on one of the days you've set for your alone time, enforce the consequence, and don't answer the door.

And that, my empath warrior, is how you set boundaries. Determine who the violators are, establish your boundaries, tell them when they break them, and if they do it again, enforce the consequences.

Build Your Own Sanctuary

A sanctuary is your safe place; when you are there, you feel reassured and peaceful. It's a space to recharge, relax, and breathe. If you live at home with your parents and there is a spare room, ask if you can use that as your sanctuary; if not, just create a space in your bedroom. Here are some tips on how to build your own sanctuary.

Go Shopping: A sanctuary is not an ordinary space; it should be full to the brim of the things you love because of how they make you feel. If you don't already have them, you will need to go shopping. Here are some things you might want to consider buying:

- Movies
- Books
- Soft blankets
- Bean bags
- Journals
- Painting or drawing supplies
- A prayer/meditation cushion
- Candles
- Headphones
- Snacks
- Religious texts if you are religious

Empath Secrets

You know what you need and like, so add or take away from this list as it suits you.

What Not to Include

When you are in your space, you need to feel totally calm and relaxed, and there are certain things that can trigger anxiety or panic attacks in empaths. For example, your phone. With all the social media apps, emails, text messages, and phone calls, keeping your phone in your sanctuary is not ideal. When you are on your way to your sanctuary, leave all the things that are not going to benefit you in another room. Additionally, to reap the full benefits of a sanctuary, you will need to clear your mind of all negativity (we will talk about that in the next chapter). Leave behind the following:

- Self-judgment
- Self-blame
- Shame
- Anxiety
- Worry

The Right Colors

The colors you have in your sanctuary are up to you, but it is also important to remember that colors evoke both positive and negative emotions:

- White: Neutrality, space, cleanliness, innocence, purity
- Black: Mourning/death, evil, strength, power, authority
- Gray: Practical, timeless, neutral
- Red: Intensity, excitement, energy, comfort, warmth, gentle, love
- Orange: Stimulation, change, enthusiasm, excitement, energetic, happy
- Yellow: Anger, frustration, intensity, hunger, optimism, warmth, cheery, laughter, happiness
- Green: Calmness, harmony, tranquillity, envy, growth, natural
- Blue: Focused, truth, uncaring, cold, serenity, calmness
- Purple: Mystery, respect, prosperity, spiritual, wisdom, sophistication
- Brown: Security, comfort, warmth, sadness, stability, reliability
- Pink: Agitation, calming, gentle, love, romance

Decorations

You can make your sanctuary even more appealing by adding some decorations to it. You might want to hang pictures of your loved ones on the wall, paintings you like, statues, flowers, or plants. Maybe you enjoy a certain ambiance like red, blue, or green lights.

Feng Shui

Feng shui is about making sure your home has the right balance of energetic balance. You will also hear this referred to as chi. Feng shui originates from China. They have been practicing it for over 3,000 years. The word feng means wind, and the word shui translates into water. For the Chinese, wind and water refer to good health. Over time the meaning has evolved, and today, it translates into good fortune. The idea of feng shui is rooted in the Taoist understanding and vision of nature. This school of thought believed that the land was full of energy and that it was alive, and they referred to it as chi.

Feng shui is basically how humans interact with their environment. It is the belief that we can manipulate the energy in our living space. By designing or positioning our surroundings, we can make sure it is in sync with the principles of the natural flow of energy.

I can testify to the fact that feng shui works; my home is feng shuid out (if that's even a word)! There are some basic principles you will need to learn before you can activate this amazing power in your house. Here are the five main elements:

Water: Water is one of the most powerful elements, and it creates the refreshing energy of harmony and ease. It gives us a sense of renewal and flow. Water also signifies abundance, and it is often used to attract wealth. The colors of the water element are black and blue. You can add water to your space with decorative pieces such as fountains, blue rugs, pictures of water, and mirrors.

Metal: Metal invokes productivity, efficiency, discipline, and structure. It also repels distractions and brings lightness, clarity, and calm. Metals colors are grey and white. Use it to give balance to areas in the home that are missing structure because they are too warm and cozy. When using metal, it's important that you use the right balance because too much can create an unwelcoming and cold atmosphere. Decorative pieces like bowls, metal frames, wall decorations, grey walls, white pillows, and rugs will add the metal element to your home.

Earth: Earth represents support, stability, protection, and nourishment. It makes you feel grounded and provides a sense of peace. Earth is an important element to add to your home because our modern lives are so stressful and hectic. The earth element expresses itself through the colors taupe, sandy, and beige, and it is particularly effective in a bedroom. You can use decorative touches such as pictures of landscapes, light yellow pillows, beige rugs, and pottery.

Fire: Fire is connected to the sun, and it creates a sense of creativity and joy. It also represents passion, romance, and love. The fire element expresses itself through the colors magenta, purple, pink, orange, yellow, and bright red. It is important to note that when it comes to fire, empaths should limit this element in their space because it's a very intense color, and it is not ideal when you are feeling overwhelmed. However, you can use it to add a pop of color with decorative pieces such as small pink or red cushions, yellow lampstands, images of fire, and candles in the colors I've just mentioned.

Wood: Wood invites growth, vitality, and health. It is also a symbol of abundance, and it is used to promote prosperity and wealth. The wood element is expressed through the colors brown and green. To incorporate wood into your home, use pictures of vegetation, green cushions or pillows, and healthy plants.

Now that you are familiar with the main principles of feng shui, the next step is to put it into practice in your home by using some of the following strategies:

Air Out: In the same way negative energy gets trapped in your body if it isn't released, it also gets trapped in the home. Even if it's freezing outside, open all the windows in the house so that all negative energy present can flow out.

Burn Incense: Burning incense sticks have been a meditation and spiritual practice for centuries. It can help raise your vibrations and amplify energy levels in your home. Nag champa creates a calm and serene atmosphere; try burning some during meditation.

Essential Oils: Orange uplifts the mood and gets rid of negative energy. The smell has a subconscious connection with the sun. You can add a few drops of orange essential oil to a spray bottle and spray it around the house.

Fix Broken Items: Broken items open the door to stuck and negative energy. If you can't fix it, get rid of it.

Declutter: Objects hold energy, which is why you typically feel stressed and tired when you are surrounded by clutter. Make sure your home is kept neat and tidy so that negative energy doesn't get stuck.

Crystals: Black tourmaline crystals repel and get rid of negative energy. Additionally, white rose quartz crystals release positive energy into the environment. Feng shui expert Christmann advises that they are kept next to electrical devices.

Smudge with Sage: Smudging your environment with sage is a Native American technique used to get rid of bad energy. Light a bunch of sage. Once it catches fire, blow it out after a couple of seconds and use the smoke to clear out your area. Experts recommend that you start at the front door and work your way around the house. As the smoke fills the atmosphere, visualize the peace and tranquillity you want in your home.

Salt: Salt absorbs negative energy. Put it in the four corners of the rooms in your home and leave it to sit for 48 hours. After that time, sweep the salt up and throw it in the trash outside your home.

Yellow Walls: Color plays an important role in your home, and interior designer Ana Zuravliova states that yellow neutralizes negative energy. Additionally, it also adds a warm tone and makes the space seem larger.

A Bell: Now, this almost sounds too good to be true, but according to psychic Melissa Mattern, ringing a bell in each corner of a room and then setting the intention for the sound waves to replace bad energy with good energy will quickly eliminate anything negative in your home.

A Good Clean: Give each room a thorough clean. Use cleaning spray to wipe down all surfaces because removing dirt will also remove negative energy.

Get Rid of Sharp Corners: According to feng shui expert Zuravilova, sharp corners invite negative energy, and round corners invite positive energy. If you have a lot of square furniture in the home, start replacing it with round objects.

More Mirrors: Infusing your house with positive energy is referred to as chi. Mirrors not only give out positive energy, but they also help cleanse the mind. Make sure they are round mirrors with no sharp edges.

Seal Your Entrances: Windows and doors are entrance points for energy. Make sure these areas are cleansed at all times. You can do this by adding white vinegar, salt, and lemon juice to a bucket of water, stir to combine, and then use the mixture to wipe down those areas. Afterward, sprinkle sea salt under the doormats; this will prevent negative energy from coming into your home.

Stick to Neutral Colors: Rich dark colors look awesome, but they are also extremely vibrant. When you are feeling overwhelmed, these are not the colors you want to be surrounded by. Dark colors make spaces look smaller than they are, so when it comes to decorating your home, stick to neutral colors like white and cream. Not only do these colors produce a calming effect, but they also make the space appear bigger.

Take an Epsom Salt Bath

I take an Epsom salt bath every evening, and I would advise that you do too. Here's why.

Relaxes the Muscles: When you are stressed out and overwhelmed, your muscles tense up. After a long, hard day surrounded by people with negative energy, soaking in an Epsom salt bath is a great way to relax your body.

Magnesium Injection: Epsom salt is high in magnesium. By soaking in it, magnesium is absorbed by the body. Magnesium deficiency causes anxiety, difficulty sleeping, and hyperactivity. This is because magnesium plays a role in the transmission of nerve impulses, energy production, and body temperature regulation.

Detoxify: Epsom salt baths help to detoxify the body. Whatever toxins or pathogens were planning on making you sick, an Epsom salt bath will stop them dead in their tracks by bringing them to the surface and expelling them before they are fully absorbed.

Grounding and Calming: A combination of the warm water, magnesium, and the yin that holds the nature of water will produce such a calming effect, that you will feel as if you are back in the womb. The elements within this bath make you feel supported and contained.

How to Take an Epsom Salt Bath

- Fill your bath with warm water, add 1–3 cups of Epsom salt. The amount of Epsom salt you use will depend on how you are feeling. The more overwhelmed you feel, add more salt.
- 1 cup of baking soda (baking soda intensifies the detoxification process; it is also good for insomnia).
- 3–6 drops of essential oils (I will talk about these shortly).
- Give the water a good whirl at the same time as releasing your intention into the water by saying out loud what you intend the Epsom bath to achieve.
- Burn some incense, light some candles, turn on some soothing music, and get a book.
- Soak in the bath for 20–30 minutes, roll up a towel, and rest your head on it.
- When you get out of the bath and pull the plug, visualize all the negative energy from the day being washed down the drain.

Empath Secrets

Essential Oils to Add to Your Bath

- **Stress Relief:** A blend of orange essence, cedarwood, clove bud, and lemon
- **Energizing:** Rosemary, sweet orange, and lemon
- **Sore muscles:** Ylang-ylang, lavender, berry, and juniper
- **Calming:** Rose absolute, lavender, and Egyptian geranium
- **Balancing:** Tea tree, mint, and sage
- **Clear your mind:** Rosemary and lemon
- **Relax:** Roman chamomile, lavender, bergamot, and clary sage

Practice Yoga

Yoga has been a massive blessing in my life. Before I got serious about my empath gift, I had no idea that negative energy can get trapped in your body. This is one of the reasons why empaths are often labeled as hypochondriacs. Additionally, it is not uncommon for us to be diagnosed with conditions such as anxiety, chronic headaches, sciatica, and chronic back pain.

Emotions are designed to flow through the body. It is the norm to express positive emotions. When we find something funny, we laugh until we cry. When we are happy about something, we can't stop smiling. When we are excited, we jump up and down. But most of us don't express negative emotions too well. We live in a world where emotions such as fear, anger, frustration, and shame are not tolerated. I was raised in a home just like this, and from a young age, I remember repressing my emotions to avoid getting told off by my parents. I developed a habit of hiding how I truly felt, and this carried on into my adult years.

What I learned during therapy was that emotions are designed to flow naturally through the body, and if they don't, they get trapped and manifest as emotional imbalance, burnout, and drained energy. Eventually, if the negative energy remains stuck, it turns into disease. Many people are immediately cured of supposedly incurable conditions through a deep tissue massage because they intercept energetic blockages and cause an emotional release. Empaths are particularly susceptible to trapped negative energy because empaths who don't understand their gifts don't know it's there. Apart from having a deep tissue massage, one of the most effective ways to release trapped energy is through yoga. Here are some poses I have found really helpful:

Savasana

The savasana is a very important pose because it requires complete stillness. There is no movement. You can use this time to process information and reflect. As well as being one of the most important poses, it is also a very difficult pose because it requires mental stillness. It is easier to be present with the other poses because you've got to focus on the pose, but with the savasana, you are just lying on your back.

- Roll out a yoga mat in the middle of the floor and put a cushion at one end to rest your head.
- Lie on your back and rest your head on the pillow.
- Spread your arms out on either side of you and part your legs slightly.
- Take slow, deep breaths.
- Allow every negative emotion you are feeling to come to the surface, and just remain present in those emotions.
- When you are ready, give yourself permission to release those negative emotions.

I always do the savasana pose first because I find that it frees my mind to flow effortlessly through the rest of the poses. I typically lie in this position until I experience an emotional release, and that is often expressed in the form of laughter, crying, or deep yawning.

Legs Against the Wall

This type of pose is referred to as a sweet release because it helps to purify the energy in the body. It allows the legs to get rid of old energy, and mentally, the heaviness slowly disappears.

- Sit in front of a wall with your legs crossed.
- Use a cushion as a headrest.
- Lie on your back, lift your legs up, and rest them against the wall.
- Scoot downwards so your bottom is touching the wall.
- Take slow, deep breaths, and focus on your breathing.
- Rest in this position until you feel an emotional release.

Supported Twist

- Use a large bolster and put a blanket over the top of it for extra support.
- Lie on your side and rest your head on the bolster.
- Your torso should be facing downwards.
- Bring your knees upwards.
- Take slow, deep breaths, and focus on it.
- Pay attention to the negative emotions you experience.
- Relax all parts of your body.
- Give yourself permission to release those emotions.

Child's Pose

When you take the position of a child, it allows you to become emotionally vulnerable, and your emotions will flow in the same way they did when you were a child.

- Put a pillow out in front of you.
- Get on your knees and lie forward so that your face is resting on the pillow.
- Put your arms on either side of the pillow.

- Take slow, deep breaths, and allow yourself to feel the negative emotions that come up.

Pigeon Pose

This hip opener pose is both mentally and physically challenging, but it is a great way to release blocked emotions.

- Put a pillow out in front of you to rest your head on.
- Sit in an upright position, resting on your knees.
- Slowly push one leg all the way backward and remain sitting on your other knee.
- Lean forward so that your torso is resting on your knee and your head is resting on the pillow.
- Put your arms out on either side of you.
- Take slow, deep breaths, and feel any negative emotions that come up.
- When you feel ready, give yourself permission to release those emotions.

Reclined Bound Angle

A lot of our emotions are stored in the hip area; when we feel threatened, we tense up this area as we prepare to operate in the fight-or-flight response. When those emotions are not processed, they stay there and cause a blockage. Additionally, this is also where the second chakra is located, and it is connected to our relationships, which is often the cause of emotions such as loss, resentment, or abandonment. When there is a restriction in this chakra, you will feel stuck and experience difficulties in your personal relationships.

- Place a bolster on the floor.
- Lie on your back so you are looking up at the ceiling.
- Stretch your arms out on either side of you.
- Bring your knees up and point them outwards.
- Put the soles of your feet together.
- Take deep, slow breaths, and feel any negative emotions that come up.
- When you feel ready, give yourself permission to release those emotions.

Breathing Exercises

Most people don't think about breathing because it's an unconscious action. We just do it. The problem isn't that we breathe unconsciously, it's that we don't breathe properly. In general, people take shallow breaths from the chest. What this does is prevents the body from getting the right amount of oxygen. To make matters worse, when we start feeling stressed, we take shallow, quick breaths. I used to have panic attacks when I got overwhelmed because I'd start breathing faster and faster, and I didn't understand why. The correct way to breathe is to take deep, slow, and shallow breaths. This helps to get more oxygen into the cells, which improves circulation, lowers blood pressure, and slows the heart rate down. The result is that you have more energy. I do breathing exercises twice a day and when I start feeling overwhelmed.

Simple Deep Breathing

- Get into a comfortable position. You can either sit or lie down.
- Inhale through your nose and fill your stomach with air.
- Exhale through your nose.
- Rest one hand on your stomach, the other on your chest.
- Feel your stomach rise as you breathe in.
- Feel your stomach deflate as you breathe out.
- Continue breathing like this for ten minutes.

Focus on Your Breath

- Sit or lie in a comfortable position and close your eyes.
- Take several deep breaths.
- As you breathe in, imagine that the air is saturated with calm and peace.
- Experience this sensation throughout your body.
- As you breathe out, imagine that the air leaving your body is the tension and stress you are feeling.
- Either say out loud, or think about a word or phrase such as "I breathe in peace of mind."
- Either say out loud, or think about a word or phrase such as "I breathe out anxiety and frustration."
- Continue this exercise for ten minutes.

Modified Lion's Breath

- Sit or lie in a comfortable position.
- Take a deep breath in through your nose and fill your stomach with air.

- Once your stomach is filled with air, open your mouth as wide as you can and make the sound, "HA" as you breathe out.
- Continue this exercise for ten minutes.

Move Away

When you enter into an environment and you are in good spirits and suddenly start feeling off, it's because you've stepped into negative energy. Because empaths are so spiritually sensitive, you will be able to sense which direction the negative energy is coming from. If you can, move into the middle of the room and pay attention to the direction that you feel the strongest negative pull. Once you are sure, make sure you stay away from that area. If the negative energy keeps getting closer to you, excuse yourself and go outside.

If you are at a movie theater, a doctor's office, public transport, or some other enclosed location, just move. When I'm in a waiting room or on public transport, I put my bag on the seat next to me to prevent anyone from sitting there. In some cases, there are no more seats and I'm forced to move my bag to allow someone to sit down, but if I start feeling negative energy, I move. If you are at a restaurant, and the table next to you is making too much noise, explain the situation to whoever you are with and ask the waiter/waitress to move you. Don't feel guilty about doing what's right for you. Empaths have a bad habit of suffering in silence, but if you are going to step into the fullness of your gift, you will need to start standing up for yourself.

Keep Physical Contact to a Minimum

Energy is transferred through touch and eyes. In general, people find it rude if you don't hug, shake hands, or kiss them on the cheek when you greet them. Oh well! When you meet someone and you don't feel comfortable, don't engage in physical contact. If a family member or a friend is in distress and they need comforting, cut the hug short so you don't pick up their energy. Also, energy transfers take place through the eyes. If you are not getting good vibes from a person, don't make eye contact with them.

Protective Meditation

Meditation is a powerful spiritual practice that will keep you centered so that you are able to live a fulfilling life as an empath. There are different types of meditation, and protective meditation is extremely beneficial for highly sensitive people. Not only does it ground you, but it helps you release the negative energy you have absorbed. I practice this every day and it does wonders for me. Additionally, you can practice it anywhere, so you can use it any time you are in an environment, and you start feeling overwhelmed.

- Focus on your breath instead of what's going on around you.
- Slowly breathe in and out and pay attention to what's going on in your body.
- Any thoughts that come, acknowledge them, but allow them to pass and keep focusing on your breath.
- Stop thinking. Just feel, breathe, and become aware of what's going on in your body.
- Take a deep breath in, and a long exhale out to release the negative energy you have absorbed.
- Breathe out stress and anxiety, breathe in peace and serenity.
- Breathe out pain and anger, breathe in contentment and calmness.
- Imagine that you are breathing toxic energy out of your lower back.
- The gap between the lumbar vertebrae are portals for releasing negative energy.

Empath Secrets

- As you continue breathing, repeat the following mantra out loud or in your head: "Transmute into positive energy."
- The words act as a command to your body, and your breath is what carries the discomfort out of your body and transforms it into positive energy so that it can go back into the universe without causing damage.

You can take this meditation even further by focusing on your heart chakra. The heart chakra is positioned in the middle of the chest. It plays an important role in compassion, love, forgiveness, empathy, relationships, and emotions. For this exercise, you will need to place your hand over your heart and focus on an image that evokes positive emotion, such as the ocean, an animal, a child's face, a rose, or a sunset. Focus on how this vision makes you feel and allow all the toxic energy to leave your body as you allow unconditional love to purify you. Repeat the mantra, "I completely release you, and allow everything negative and unhealthy to leave my body."

I often feel unwanted emotions in a certain part of my body, such as my stomach. In such instances, I will place my hand over my stomach and send positive energy there. At the end of your meditation session, thank the divine forces of healing and the universe for giving you the power to clear negative energy. Trust that your body is now healthy, whole, clear, and purified. You are powerful and strong, and you are fully equipped to take on the world.

Positive Empath Affirmations

Affirmations are positive statements that you repeat to yourself to silence that negative inner voice. However, affirmations are more than just words. Research suggests that they promote self-confidence and give people the courage to believe in themselves. They help the conscious mind shift the focus from negative self-beliefs to positive self-beliefs. I am not going to go into the exact science behind this because it will probably bore you. But what I can say is that positive affirmations are not some sort of miracle cure. If you are going to reap the benefits of using affirmations, you will need to back up everything you are saying with actions. You've only got to read some of the self-help books out there to discover that a lot of fairy tales have been sold to the public about affirmations. The assumption is that you can just stand in front of the mirror and tell yourself things, and they will start showing up in your life. Not so, my friend! No action equals no manifestation. I have said this several times throughout the book, and I will say it again: If you want to truly connect with your empath gift, you've got to put the work in. Here are the affirmations I have been saying out loud every day since I started on this journey:

- I release every feeling that doesn't belong to me.
- I don't need to fix the issues I can sense coming from other people.
- I wear my gifts with honor, I am an empath, and I am proud.
- I embrace my sensitive nature.
- I will always take time out to recharge and rest.
- I do not hide my needs because I deserve the same respect as everyone else.
- I protect my energy at all times.

Neutralize Energy Vampires: Energy vampires are people who suck the life out of you. They love empaths because we are so willing to give them what they want. In your private life, you can either cut such people out or set boundaries, but in a work environment, it's a bit more difficult. But there are ways you can keep them at arm's length. Gandhi said a very fitting quote: "I will not allow anyone to walk through my mind with their dirty feet." If you want to keep your sanity, it's essential that you take on the same approach. If you work in an office, you can start by putting a sign on your door or on your desk saying something like, *Energy Vampires Are Not Welcome Here.* This sign will let the energy vampires know that if they are going to interact with you, it needs to be in a positive way, or they can kick rocks!

Another strategy is to use your positive energy as a superpower to zap them out of your way. Every time they say something negative, respond with a positive statement. Energy vampires hate positive energy because it reminds them of how negative they are, and this makes them feel uncomfortable. It's basically shining a light on the places they don't want to deal with. You can compare it to exposing a vampire to daylight; their response is to run and hide somewhere dark because that is where they are safe. An energy vampire is no different. If you can keep zapping them with your positive energy, it will only be a matter of time before they stop bothering you.

Cut Etheric Cords

As you know, toxic people love empaths. Our power is so healing and loving that they love to bask in our energy, and we let them. But as a result, we form etheric cords with these people, which is one of the main reasons why we keep allowing them to come back into our lives no matter how bad they make us feel. So what are etheric cords? We are born with them. You will also hear them referred to as ribbons, energy cords, ethereal cords, and cords of attachment. They are energy structures that are connected to your chakras and auras and extend out of you. They connect with things like past events, situations, objects, animals, places, and people. When you cord with someone, you feel a connection with that person, and this is how you tap into their energy. Do you sometimes feel that you know what the people closest to you are thinking or feeling? That's probably because of the etheric cord.

Etheric cords are necessary to build healthy relationships and to connect with your environment. However, when you make connections with toxic people, this becomes a problem. Outside of the people who are currently in your life, I am sure there are relationships you've had with toxic people that you no longer speak to, but you still have a deep connection with them. This might be because you have an etheric attachment with them, and you are still sending and receiving energy to and from that person.

When you are corded to a negative person, you feel drained just from being in their presence. They don't even need to say or do anything. This is because the cord is sending you negative energy and taking energy from you at the same time. One of the most obvious signs that you are corded with someone is when you can't stop thinking about them.

How Do Etheric Cords Work?: Etheric cords can attach anywhere on the body, but there are some areas that are more common than others. The solar plexus chakra plays an important role in your personal power. It is located in the pit of your stomach. Also, they can attach to your lower stomach. This is where your sacral chakra is located, and it is responsible for your emotions and sex life. You will find that these cords are connected to your romantic partners. You will start receiving energetic information from them once you are connected. The more you get to know this person, the stronger the cord becomes, which makes it easier to connect to their energy field. When I found out about etheric cords, I had to cut many, but the first was with my ex-husband. I had to make sure it was completely severed to prevent him from ever coming back into my life again.

How to Cut Etheric Cords: Cutting etheric cords isn't something you do once. You will need to participate in this ritual often. Because guess what? When one cord is cut, another one shows up, and that's because we are constantly meeting new people. I have incorporated cutting etheric cords into my nightly routine because every day, I come into contact with at least one person with toxic energy. There are a number of ways you can cut etheric cords, here are some of them:

Cord Cutting Through a Ritual

- Make sure you are alone and that no one is going to disturb you.
- Sit or lie down in a comfortable position and start taking deep breaths to relax your body and mind.
- Once you are fully relaxed, invite your protective angels and spirit guides to guide you through the ritual (we will discuss this in Chapter Five).
- I invite them by repeating the following mantra: "Hello, protective angels and spirit guides. I am summoning you to assist me in breaking free

from all negative connections. Give me the power to cut loose from all the attachments that are draining me and having a negative influence on my life. Protect my attachment of happiness and love but free me from all negative attachments from this person(s) (name them) from now until eternity."

- Keep repeating this mantra throughout the ritual.
- While you are chanting, imagine a large angelic sword cutting the cord.
- Thank your protective angels and spirit guides for cutting the cords.
- Take an Epsom salt bath after you have completed the ritual.
- You will know the ritual has worked because you will feel lighter.
- Drink plenty of water to replenish your body.

Cord Cutting Through Meditation

If you are going to incorporate meditation into your daily routine, you can also cut etheric cords at the same time. Once you have completed your meditation session, visualize all the cords that are attached to you and invite your protective angels and spirit guides to assist you by repeating the mantra mentioned above. Ask them to cut all the negative cords attached to you and protect the positive cords.

Cord Cutting Through Visualization

If you don't have time to go through the full cord cutting ritual, you can also do it by visualization before going to bed. Once you've got into a relaxed state, visualize the etheric cords that are extending from you. Look out for any thin and dull cords; the thin cords come from the interactions you have with people throughout the day. The dull cords are the strong negative cords you have formed with people over time. Visualize your angelic forces and spirit guides using their swords to cut them.

Cord Cutting Through Prayer

You can pray at any time throughout the day. You don't need to speak out loud; a quiet whisper is enough. You can either chant the cord-cutting mantra, or you can pray to your spirit guides and angels and ask them to help you cut any negative cords. I don't think cutting cords through prayer is as effective, but it helps when you have just left a crowded environment. I usually say a quick prayer after I've left a party, restaurant, or shopping mall. Basically, anywhere there are a lot of people. I will then perform the full ritual once I get home.

Cord Cutting with an Energy Healer

If you find visualization difficult, then I would advise you to go to an energy healer. I visited one every month for a full year when I first started on my journey because I had such a strong bond with my husband. Energy healers are experts, and they have been thoroughly trained in this area. They know how to reset the energy field around your body.

Visualize Protecting Your Energy

Shielding visualization is a powerful way to protect yourself against negative energy at the same time as allowing a free flow of positive energy. Shielding takes some practice to master, but once you get it, you won't regret the effort you put into perfecting it. I use this technique several times throughout the day; I practice it first thing in the morning, and I use it as soon as I walk into a situation and start feeling uncomfortable.

Empath Secrets

This could be when I'm speaking to an energy vampire, in a crowded restaurant, in traffic, or in a packed waiting room. Here are the steps you will need to take:

- Take some deep, long breaths.
- Visualize a beautiful pink or white light, or a shield surrounding your body.
- This shield is your protection. It won't allow anything negative to come near you.
- Because you know you are protected, it makes you feel energized, centered, and happy.
- Not only are you protected against negativity, but you can also feel the love and positive vibes in your environment.

There is so much more to protecting yourself as an empath, but as I've mentioned, there is such an avalanche of information out there that it can become overwhelming. What I have provided is enough to get you started, but you will grow as you go. Some of the strategies you might not use, but it's all about finding what works best for you. Now that you know how to protect your energy, it's time to really get familiar with your empath gift and step into your superpower abilities.

Takeaways

- You've got to protect your energy at all costs. A strong energy field will ensure that you are capable of operating at your full potential. You can do this by setting boundaries and letting people know that they can't have access to you when they want.
- Your environment should radiate positive energy. You may need to give your home a good clean so that negative energy doesn't get trapped and stay in your abode longer than it needs to.
- Cord-cutting ensures that you don't remain connected to the people who are sending their negative energy to you and draining you of your positive energy.
- Additionally, you can practice yoga, take an Epsom salt bath, and meditate to rid yourself of negative energy and ground yourself. Visualization and saying positive affirmations are also powerful ways to protect your energy.

Chapter 5: How to Awaken Your Superpower and Operate in the Fullness of Your Calling

"Empathy is the medicine the world needs." ~ Judith Orloff

Every gifted person has a superpower, but if that superpower is never developed, it won't reach its full potential. Usain Bolt knew he had a sprinting ability at the age of 14. His gift began to attract attention at school, and he was trained by former Olympic sprint athlete Pablo McNeil. He won several high school championships and took to the world stage in 2002 when he received a gold medal for the 200-meter dash at the World Junior Championships in Kingston. Today he is known as an Olympic legend, he has won many accolades, and he has been referred to as "the fastest man alive." Despite his natural ability, Usain Bolt has a rigorous training schedule and a very strict diet. He works out for 90 minutes a day in the gym, plus additional training when he is preparing for a 100- or 200-meter sprint. He also eats a strict diet loaded with superfoods that help fight muscle inflammation and boost energy.

Why does Usain Bolt train and eat like this when he was born with a sprinting ability? His gift is his body; he runs with his legs. If his body is not maintained through diet and exercise, it is going to hinder his ability to perform at his best. If his muscle was to turn into fat, it would be absolutely impossible for him to run at the speed that he does. So, what has Usain Bolt got to do with you when you're an empath? Well, before I knew I was an empath, I was all over the place, and as you read in the introduction, I was in and out of abusive relationships my entire life. I just couldn't get it together. Why? Because I didn't know I had a gift that would work against me if I didn't know how to manage it. But as soon as I started applying the techniques that my therapist introduced me to, everything changed for me. But I didn't stop once I got to a certain level. To this day, I still practice these techniques to enhance my gift. If you are going to operate in the fullness of your calling, practice is essential, so here are some tips to get you started.

Empath Secrets

Get Supernatural Help

Empaths are supernatural beings, and we are deeply connected with the spiritual realm. I've seen ghosts all my life. My parents used to tell me to stop being so ridiculous, but I could see them just as I could see humans. I was never scared of them; they were my friends. A woman I called the "bag lady" would visit me at night. She was always carrying a bag. She would sit on the end of my bed and talk to me about her husband with incredible sadness in her eyes. She came to see me every night for three years and then one night I never saw her again. I would call for her; "Bag lady, bag lady," I whispered, but nothing! She didn't come back, but I always thought of her. In my later years, when I started learning about my gift, I did some research on my old house. I found out that a lady called Mrs. Cooper had committed suicide in my room. She was found with a bag full of pictures and some clothing items that belonged to her dead husband. He died in a car accident a few months before she took her life. You've probably had supernatural encounters, too; don't dismiss them. The spirit world wants to connect with you.

Whether "normal" people want to acknowledge it or not, everyone has a spirit guide; they are assigned to us before we came to the earth. You see, before we were formed in the womb, we were spirits. The spirit world knows exactly who we are, even if we don't know who they are. As you go throughout your life, they walk with you, and sometimes other spirit guides are sent when you need more help than normal. Your spirit guides are like a team, and they include:

Archangels: Archangels are at the top of the food chain; they have the most powerful energy fields of all angels. When I call on an archangel, I feel a definite energy shift in the room, similar to what I felt any time I saw a ghost. Every archangel holds expertise in a certain area. For example, the archangel Raphael is a healing angel, and he can work with more than one human at a time.

Guardian Angels: Guardian angels belong to you alone; their sole purpose is to assist you with your earthly assignment. They are totally devoted to you and love you unconditionally. You can call on your guardian angels anytime you need immediate assistance.

Helper Angels: You could compare helper angels to freelancers; they don't have a specific assignment but go where the work is. They show up when you are least expecting them, such as while you are looking for a new office space. Or you might have had to cut off some friends, and now you're feeling lonely, so a helper angel might come to help you look for new friends.

Spirit Animals: A spirit animal can be a pet who died and returned to the spirit world, or an animal that has been sent to teach you something. All animals represent something. Wolves are sent to teach you about the importance of survival. Peacocks are sent to teach you about confidence. Pay attention to animals you see a lot. You might see them in your dreams, on a friend's coffee mug, or in your backyard.

Deceased Loved Ones: Loved ones who have passed on into the spirit realm might decide to join your team of spirit guides in helping you fulfill your earthly duties. Grandmothers are often known to be important spirit guides who send their loved ones wisdom and help them make important life decisions. Anyone who dies can become your spirit guide. I believe the bag lady was my spirit guide, but because I didn't know anything about the spiritual realm at that point, I didn't ask her for anything. Or let's say you are a gifted dancer. A dead person who was a dancer when they were alive might choose to help guide you to the right opportunities to take your career to the next level.

Ascended Masters: Influential people like Martin Luther King Jr., Mother Theresa, or Mahatma Gandhi might choose to be your spirit guide. My spirit guides have told me that ascended masters work together in the spirit realm no matter their culture or religious beliefs when they were alive. On the other side, those things don't matter.

Your Spirit Guides and How They Communicate with You

Coincidences: I have never believed in coincidences, and now that I have a better understanding of spirit guides, I know why. One of the ways they speak to you is through coincidences. For example, after I divorced my husband, and spent a few years single while I got myself together, I met the wonderful man I am married to now. A year or so into our relationship, we started having problems, and one night before bed, we had a blazing row. I went to sleep thinking this man is awesome, but we don't seem to be able to communicate very well. The next day while I was on my way to work, I was thinking about leaving him. When I got to the office, I made my way to the canteen to grab a coffee, and there was a book on the table about how to communicate effectively with your romantic partner. I scooped that book up and devoured every page. I gave the book to my partner to read, and we both made the decision to implement the strategies in the book. Needless to say, we got married a year later, and we are still together, and our ability to communicate with each other just keeps getting better and better.

Numbers: Spirit guides communicate to you through numbers and sequences of numbers because they have special meanings. If you've got a lucky number, you might find that it keeps showing up after you've made an important decision, and your spirit guides are letting you know that you've made the right choice.

- 1: The number 1 means you need to develop a deeper trust in your ability to succeed. You will keep seeing the number 1 when you are about to start a new chapter in your life, such as start a new job or launch a business.

- 2: The number 2 represents self-reflection. Take some time out to think about the direction your life is heading, and the goals you need to set to accomplish your mission. Also, the number 2 is a sign that people are pressuring you to go in the wrong direction and that you need to trust your instincts more.
- 3: The number 3 means that you need to embrace something, you might be holding back from starting something new, or you could be holding back from speaking the truth about something.
- 4: The number 4 means that there is something lacking in your life, you may be neglecting relationships, or neglecting yourself.
- 5: The number 5 means that you need to make a change when you feel as if you are stuck in a rut, or things are just not moving for you. Repeated stagnation is often a sign you need to take a different course of action.
- 6: The number 6 is related to balance, especially work-life balance. You are either spending too much time with friends and family and not focusing on getting the raise you need to make life better for your future, or you are spending

too much time at work and not enough time with your family.

- 7: The number 7 means that you need to take some time out. You might need to take a trip on your own somewhere to reconnect with who you are and your life's purpose.
- 8: The number 8 is an indication that you are going to overcome the challenges you are facing. It's a sign that you need to look for treasure in a dark place
- 9: The number 9 is a sign of compassion. You either need to treat yourself better or treat other people better.
- 0: The number 0 symbolizes infinity. It is a sign that you have reached a deep level of spirituality or that you are being your authentic self and refusing to live according to anyone else's standards. You can take it as a sign that you are doing the right thing.

Number Sequences: When you see a sequence of numbers, it means something even more powerful than seeing one number. For example, two numbers are more powerful than one, three more powerful than two, etc.

- 11, 111, 1111: The number 1 sequence is often seen when a person has been given the opportunity to share their gift. It could be through teaching or a performance. Multiple 1s is a sign that your intuition is at its peak, and you have a lot of inspiration to tap into.
- 22, 222, 2222: The number 2 sequence means that it's time to start breathing life into your vision. If you've been planning for a while and have not started putting things together, this number sequence is giving you the green light to go ahead. Additionally, it means that you are about to reap what you have sown, so don't give up.
- 33, 333, 3333: The number 3 sequence is a representation of communication and sharing. It is often a sign that you need to start being more open with someone in your life. It also means that you have an important message to deliver to the world.
- 44, 444, 4444: The number 4 sequence means that the universe is testing you. It appears as if things are not moving in the direction you want because of the obstacles and roadblocks you are facing, but they are tests, and there is a lesson in what you are

going through. The number 4 sequence is also a warning that tests are on the way and that you should prepare for adversity.

- 55, 555, 5555: The number 5 sequence is a sign that you need to move away from something. You might be in a toxic relationship, or your friends are energy vampires, or you are no longer satisfied with your job. Basically, the number 5 sequence is a sign that you need to cut ties with everything that is not serving you.
- 66, 666, 6666: The number 6 sequence is a sign that you need to develop your self-esteem. You might have just come out of a bad relationship, or you are spending too much time looking in the mirror complaining about your body. It means you need to do something to boost your self-esteem because you place too much value on what people think about you.
- 77, 777, 7777: The number 7 sequence is a sign that you need to take a look at what you really want out of life. It may be that you are hanging on to parts of your life that you have outgrown, and it's time to let them go. The number 7 sequence is also a sign that you are

vibrating on a low frequency, and making a plan to move forward would increase your vibrations.

- 88, 888, 8888: The number 8 sequence is a sign that you are taking on too many of other people's problems. They are also a sign that you've got fingers in too many pies, which means you are finding it difficult to gain mastery over any one thing.
- 99, 999, 9999: The number 9 sequence is a sign that something is coming to an end. It could mean you are about to lose something, or that you are stepping out of the old and into something new. This number sequence is a gentle reminder that you need to disconnect from the past, whether it's negative emotions such as sadness, anger or resentment, or people.
- 0, 00, 000, 0000: The number 0 sequence is a sign that something has come full circle in your life, and you are about to enter into a new season. It's important that you fully trust your intuition during this time, even if things don't make sense.

Sensing a Presence: I know when my spirit guide is around because I feel a presence. This is especially true when I'm writing. It is at that point that I go into "flow mode." During this time, I can write for a good couple of hours nonstop. The only way I can describe it is that I have a river of words traveling through my fingers. A lot of empaths are creative in some way, and your spirit guides will often turn up during the creative process to guide you. You will also sense the presence of your spirit guides when you are trying to come up with a solution to a problem, or you are communicating something important to others.

Change Your Diet

In the same way a talented athlete can't maintain their gift if they live off fast and processed foods, neither can you. A clean diet isn't about losing weight, it's about ensuring that you are in your best state both physically and mentally so that you can operate at your full potential at all times. My diet has always been bad. I have a sweet tooth; cookies, chocolates, and cakes were my go-to comfort foods any time I felt depressed (which was often, by the way). I also loved junk food, and my freezer was packed with pizzas, burgers, and French fries. I had no idea that food was a major part of my problem until I started reading about it. I have been on a plant-based diet for three years, and the transformation has been tremendous. I feel lighter, my mind is clearer, I've got tons of energy, and the bonus is that I look better.

It is important to understand that everything is energy, and that includes food. Every Sunday, my ex-husband and I would go and have dinner at his mother's house. She was an angry and bitter woman who had nothing good to say. I hated going there but went for the sake of my husband. To everyone else, she was a brilliant cook. People loved her food, and relatives would flock to her house at Thanksgiving to eat her delicious meals. But I hated her food. I thought it tasted like cardboard, and every Sunday, I would force myself to eat it. I could never understand why I hated her food so much until I learned about food and energy. As I mentioned, my ex-mother-in-law was an angry woman, so no matter what ingredients she used, my sensitive nature picked up on the angry energy in the food, and that's why I hated it.

When you buy fast food, you are eating the energy of greed. When you eat food that contains pesticides, you are eating the energy of death. When you eat food prepared by an anxious person, you are eating the energy of anxiety. A lot of empaths are vegetarians because they can feel the energy from the torture the animals endured when they were killed. On the other hand, when you eat organic foods, you are eating the positive energy of a farmer who cares about the food they are selling to others. Organic, raw, no gluten, and foods that don't contain refined sugars all have a high vibration. However, it's also important that these foods are cooked by the right people, or it defeats the purpose of eating healthy food. For this reason, I no longer go to restaurants because you just don't know who is in the kitchen. I would also like to stress how important it is to drink plenty of water throughout the day. Not only does it help flush out unwanted energy, but dehydration also causes emotional stress such as panic attacks and anxiety. Here is a list of foods you should eat, and foods you should avoid:

Foods to Eat: Leafy greens, sauerkraut, kimchi, kombucha, probiotic yogurt, fruits, whole grains, quinoa, nuts and seeds, raw cacao.

Foods to Avoid: All processed foods, all junk foods, all foods high in sugar, soda, alcohol, fried foods, potato chips, energy drinks, sports drinks.

Stop Playing the Victim

"Woe is me; woe is me" used to be my battle cry. I truly believed I was a victim, and I refused to take responsibility for my life. I blamed my parents for suppressing my emotions, my partners for abusing me, and my friends for draining my energy. But this attitude didn't get me anywhere. My complaints were like one big shovel, and every time I made one, I just kept on digging deeper and deeper into a ditch of negativity that I was never going to be able to pull myself out of if I continued. Unfortunately, it is not uncommon for people to throw away every gift they have been blessed with because of the victim mentality. The bottom line is that life isn't fair, and some of us are dealt a bad hand. The question is whether you are going to play this game we call life with the hand you've been given, or are you going to surrender to it? You can overcome the victim mentality if you want to. Here are a few tips:

Find the Root Cause: Why do you feel like a victim? What happened in your childhood, your teenage years, or your adult life that caused you to adopt this mentality? You might need professional help to get to this point, but it is necessary for your complete healing. Additionally, the victim mentality is rooted in learned helplessness. Maybe you were brought up in an environment that didn't celebrate independence; instead, you were encouraged to be dependent. A consequence of this is that you didn't have the confidence to fend for yourself.

Change the Script: I spent the majority of my life playing the script of self-pity in my mind, and it was on repeat 24/7. There is nothing wrong with going through a bad situation and feeling sorry for yourself for a season. It's natural to feel depressed or sad after you've been through a traumatic event. The issue is that mourning isn't supposed to be permanent; grieve and then keep it moving. The problem is that feeling sorry for yourself feels good, and this leads to it becoming a habit. Self-pity is a defense mechanism. It makes you feel protected and numbs the pain. The reality is that over the long term, this way of thinking causes more damage than the pain you are trying to escape.

Self-pity is a choice. It's not about what happened, and it's not about the fact that you are a casualty of an attack. It's about you choosing to play the victim because it separates you from reality. You will never achieve anything when you are playing the victim. It places a secure barrier between you and the life you want to live. Self-pity is the opposite of self-reflection; it makes you invisible and puts the attention on everyone else. Not only is everyone to blame for your circumstances, but you also expect them to be the cure. When self-pity becomes the dominant force in your life, you refuse to take any responsibility for it.

The question is, how do you change the script and stop feeling sorry for yourself? It starts with awareness; as you are reading this, you will recognize yourself. That is the first step to becoming self aware. You now know that you are playing the victim, that you feel sorry for yourself, and that it feels good because it numbs the pain. The next step is to change the story you keep saying to yourself. At this stage, I would like you to get a pen and paper and write this down:

"I choose not to remain a victim; instead, I am a victor of my circumstances, I am a survivor, an overcomer, and I will use what has happened to me for the greater good."

In one sentence, you've just changed your entire life story. You have admitted you were a victim, but now you are going to use your story of victimhood for the greater good of humanity. How you choose to do that is up to you, but do it you must. Self-pity takes place in the mind. To change the script, stop entertaining thoughts of self-pity. They are renting out space in your brain, and they don't belong there, so get rid of them by repeating the sentence I've just told you to write down. It will help you to carry it around with you. Eventually, you will remember it by heart. Keep saying this until it becomes a habit. Like affirmations, it is going to feel weird at first. Your subconscious mind is going to reject it because that is not what it's familiar with.

Volunteer: You might not feel ready to take this step yet because it involves being around people who have suffered trauma. But as soon as you are ready, I highly recommend it. I volunteered in a children's hospital; it was terrible the way these innocent children suffered. Many of them had incurable diseases and only a short time to live, but they were happy and strong. I was deeply inspired, and I loved being around these children. They were suffering in a way that I couldn't imagine—the physical and mental anguish of knowing that your life is being sucked away by a disease that you have no control over. They were not like other children who could go outside, run, play, and have fun with their friends, and they knew it.

What volunteering does is get you to step outside of yourself and focus on other people less fortunate than you. What happens when you play the victim is that you start believing you are the only person in the world suffering. You might witness suffering on the TV, but you are so far removed from it that it doesn't resonate with you in that way. But when you come into contact with suffering and realize that you can make that person's life better, even if it's for a couple of hours a week, you will quickly stop feeling sorry for yourself.

Practice Gratitude: Gratitude is a powerful technique that gets you to stop focusing on what you don't have and keeps your mind fixed on what you do have. Victims are blinded by their experiences; their judgment is clouded, and it prevents them from seeing all the other beautiful things they are surrounded by. You can practice gratitude by doing the following:

- Write down five things you are grateful for right now
- Think about these things and feel the emotions associated with gratitude
- Remain in that state for at least five minutes

Repeat this exercise twice a day, first thing in the morning and before you go to bed at night. I would advise that you keep a gratitude journal on your bedside table; this will help you to remember.

Forgiveness: Playing the victim involves blaming someone/people for your current state. For me, I spent many years angry with my parents for not allowing me to express myself in the right way. I was also angry at them for not knowing who I really was. I didn't understand how they could bring me into the world and not know that I had this gift. But the more I evaluated my parents' characters, I realized that they could only raise me with the tools they had been given by their parents. They went through the same thing I did. Their parents stifled their voices, and they weren't allowed to express themselves either. During those days, children were seen and not heard, and it led to a generation of emotionally damaged children growing into adulthood, having children, and trying to raise them the best way they knew how. Once I was armed with this information, it made forgiveness a lot easier for me. Hurt people hurt people; and furthermore, how were they to know what an empath was? The term isn't popular now, and it definitely hadn't gained any traction when I was growing up.

Once you have freed yourself from the chains of unforgiveness, you will be able to move forward and start letting go of the things that are not serving you. Please note, forgiveness doesn't mean that you become best friends with the person who hurt you. It doesn't even require that you make contact and tell them they've been forgiven. Simply release the person mentally. Stop holding them hostage for something you think they are responsible for.

Sharpen Your Intuition

Every human being on the planet is intuitive by nature; it's how we were created. But empaths are more sensitive to it, which is why you can immediately walk into a room and sense that something is not right. The problem with intuition is that it doesn't scream at you. It's gentle and soft, which is why it's easy to miss. Over the years, intuition has caught the attention of scientists, and there has been a lot of research about it. One study conducted by a group of researchers at Leeds University discovered that intuition is a psychological process that involves the brain making decisions based on the information it gathers from the past, including the environment, cues, and previous experiences. The thought process takes place so quickly that the person is not consciously aware of it.

You could say that the brain operates on two different levels. You have the part that runs on instinct—it just knows what it's supposed to do, and does it. Then you have the part of the brain that is more deliberate and calculated, the part that thinks about everything before carrying out an action.

There is plenty of scientific evidence that supports the existence of intuition. One study found that the intuitive part of the brain is aware of the correct answer to something long before the part of the brain that evaluates everything. The study involved participants playing a card game that they were not aware was rigged. They had to choose from one of two card decks. One was fixed so that participants hit big wins, then big losses. The other deck of cards was fixed so that it had mostly small gains but very few losses. The participants stated that after playing 50 cards, they felt they knew which deck was the safest. After they had played 80 cards, they were confident that they could talk about the differences between the two decks. What was interesting about this study was that after they had played ten cards, whenever they picked cards from the bad deck, the sweat glands in their hands started opening. It was at this point that the participants developed a preference for the safer deck, but they were not consciously aware of it. Their intuition had started guiding them towards a better decision before they were consciously aware of what was going on.

I said all that to say this: Despite the fact that empaths are naturally intuitive, we know without a shadow of a doubt when something is off. But because we are not fully connected with our gift, we do the most ridiculous things. I can testify to this; let me give you an example. Several years ago, I had this "friend" (we will call her Julie), who was always asking me for money. She was a single mother with a part-time job, and she was struggling. Even though I had the money to spare, something just didn't feel right when I was giving it to her. Well, as empaths do, I kept giving and giving until one day, I got a phone call from another friend telling me that Julie was in jail for driving under the influence. It turns out that Julie had a drug problem, which was why she was always asking me for money. Now, I'm not knocking her for having a habit. It can happen to the best of us. I'm knocking myself for assisting her in that habit. If I had listened to my intuition, I wouldn't have felt so guilty when I heard she had been arrested. Because guess what? She had literally just called and asked for money an hour before her arrest! So she used the money I had given her to buy the drugs that she took before getting behind the wheel. It all worked out in the end, as going to jail ended up being the best thing for her. She got clean and now travels around the country speaking about the dangers of drug addiction. But she may have kicked the habit a lot earlier if I wasn't enabling her. Anyway, here are some tips on how to sharpen your intuition:

Be Quiet and Listen: Raise your hand if you enjoy trying to have a conversation in a loud room. I am assuming no one raised their hand. That's because it's difficult to be heard when there's too much noise and no one likes shouting. Your intuition doesn't shout. It's a still small voice. When it's trying to tell you something, it doesn't increase the volume of its voice. Your intuition will keep trying to nudge you in the right direction by repeating itself. Get still and listen. Meditation is a great way to do this.

Let Go of Bad Feelings: Negative emotions will stifle your intuition. This is why we make bad decisions when we are angry or upset. Research proves this. One study found that participants made better intuitive decisions in a word task when they were in a good mood as opposed to when they were in a bad mood. The moral of the story is before you are about to make a decision, make sure you are in the right frame of mind.

Accept How You Feel: When you allow yourself to feel, you will know when your intuition is at work. Some of the physical manifestations of intuition are goosebumps on the skin, you will start breathing faster, your heart will start beating louder, you will feel a shiver down your spine, or you will get butterflies in your stomach. There are times when it's really subtle, but you just know it's the right or wrong thing to do. For me, when something isn't right, I start feeling anxious. What made accepting how I felt difficult was that I felt the same anxious feeling when I was making the right decision. I had to pay attention to what my mind was telling me during both. When I was doing the right thing, there was no negative voice in my head telling me I was doing the wrong thing. But when I was doing the wrong thing, I experienced constant negative chatter in my mind. My advice is to pay attention to how you feel and write these feelings down. Over time, you will get familiar with them.

Get Selective with Your Friends: When I started on this journey, I literally had to cut off all my friends. The sad thing is that they were really nice people, they just had terrible energy. Anytime I was with them or spoke to them over the phone, I felt exhausted and drained. I literally couldn't stand being around them, and people like this will add to the noise in your head. When you don't feel good because you've been suffocated by someone's negative energy, that's all you can focus on, and there's no way you're listening out for a still, small voice. I understand that there are some people you just can't walk away from, like family members, but keep them at arm's length and don't let them get too close.

When I first started operating in my gift, I realized that my sister was a complete narcissist, and she lied all the time. So one day, I confronted her about her lies, and she hasn't spoken to me since. I had always known she was a liar, but because I didn't like confrontation, I refused to pull her up on it. One of the things that will happen when you start connecting with your gift is you will get bold. When the people surrounding you have character flaws, you will start letting them know. They are either going to respect you for it and change, or, like my sister, they will cut themselves out of your life. As the saying goes, you can choose your friends, but you can't choose your family. My sister will always be family, but until she decides to turn her life around, our relationship will remain as it is.

Trust Your Gut: According to scientific research, intuition and emotion coexist together in the gut. You will often hear the gut referred to as the second brain. That's because the gut has a lining of neurons attached to it, and they are very sensitive. This is why we feel sick when we've got an important decision to make, or when we know we've made a bad decision.

Access Your Intuition Through Iceberg Visualization

An iceberg is a large block of ice buried beneath the water, the only part that is visible to those on the ground level is the tip. I want you to imagine that you are an iceberg; the tip is everything you can think about or bring to your remembrance right now. Your unconscious mind is the largest part of the iceberg, the part you can't see. It is filled with everything you have ever seen or heard your entire life. You rarely pay attention to this part of your mind, but it shows up often in the form of a still, small voice throughout the day. Let's say you are on your way somewhere, and you are not sure of the direction. You sense that you should go left, but you go right and run into a dead end. When you realize you are at a dead end, you think to yourself, *I knew I should have turned left*.

Although your subconscious mind and your conscious mind appear to exist as separate entities, they are all one. In the sea, there are many icebergs. Although they stand alone, they are all connected because they were formed from the same water they float in.

Everything the iceberg needs to survive is in the water, and everything you need to survive is in your subconscious mind. The answer to every question you have is buried in your subconscious mind. You have full access to it, and you need to break through that barrier that is preventing you from accessing your subconscious mind. You can achieve this through visualization:

- Sit or lie in a comfortable position and take deep, slow breaths.
- Once you have reached a state of relaxation, visualize the iceberg, and imagine that you are floating in its energy.
- Continue breathing deeply and relax further.
- Imagine that you are relaxing in the water. You trust the water because you can draw from it at any time. You can release your desires into it and melt into it.
- Continue this exercise for five minutes.

As you use this visualization each day, you will start feeling a deeper connection with your subconscious mind and the world around you. Also, throughout your day, visualize the people you connect with as icebergs and tap into the energetic connection between you.

How to Transmute Negative Energy

Transmuting negative energy means transforming it into positive energy. It's important to do this because just sending the negative energy back into the universe is counterproductive. As empaths, we have the power to rid this world of everything that doesn't serve us. You can't fight fire with fire. Yes, it's true that we hate negative energy, but the only way we can eliminate it from the world is to change it, and here are a few ways you can do this.

Transmute Through Shielding

I have found transmuting negative energy through shielding extremely helpful when I'm in an environment where there is no easy escape root, such as public transport. You might be stuck in traffic, or on a train that has stopped in a tunnel.

Empath Secrets

I start by taking a few deep breaths to relax my body. I then imagine a powerful glass shield surrounding my body. As the negative energy comes my way, I set my intention, that as the negative energy makes contact with the shield, it is transmuted into peaceful, positive energy before it is sent back into the universe. When I explain this technique, I am often asked why I don't redirect the positive energy to the person who is radiating negative energy. This is a good question, and the answer is that not everyone is ready to receive positive energy. Think about it like this. It would make zero sense to pour water into a cup that is already full. You've got to empty out what's already in it first. The same principle applies to a person carrying negative energy. They've got to get rid of it first before they can receive the positive energy. So by me sending it to them, it would be a waste. Instead, I release it into the universe and set the intention that the positive energy is sent to a person who is ready to receive it.

When you are not prepared, it's easy to experience an energetic attack. This is when you were too late to shield yourself, and the negative energy has already entered your field. To begin, I imagine that my feet have drains like a sink at the bottom of them. I pull the plug out and allow the negative energy I am feeling to flow through like water into the earth beneath me. As the energy is making its way out, I visualize it transforming into healing energy for the universe

How to Transmute Your Own Negative Energy

It is also important to mention that negative energy is not just about the people you are surrounded by. It can also come from you, so here are some tips on how to transmute your own negative energy into positive solutions.

Hop onto the Energy Bus: I mentioned how important it is to stop complaining in a previous chapter but here, I want to take it a little further. Complaining is basically making noise about something without finding a solution. The complaint you have isn't the issue, the issue is that you are throwing out negative energy without releasing something positive to eradicate it. Let's say you have a problem with your manager. He/she is a micromanager; they literally stand over your shoulder and watch you do everything. The slightest little mistake you make, they bring it to your attention, and as far as they are concerned, you can never do anything right. Instead of having a nagging session with your friends over coffee, come up with a solution to the problem.

Start by evaluating yourself. Micromanagers can be annoying, but sometimes their behavior is fully justified because their employees consistently produce tardy work. Take an honest look at your work performance and determine whether you are guilty of tardiness. Do you turn up late for work? Do you miss deadlines? It could be that your manager is reacting to a legitimate concern he/she has about your work ethic. As well as self-reflection, it would also help if you had a word with your manager to ask if there is anything you can improve on.

It will probably take a bit more digging to get to the root of the problem, but once you've got it, implement it, and see if that makes a difference.

You Are Not in Control: One of the many problems that empaths find difficult is their inability to control things. It is not uncommon to believe that your life is spinning out of control. This is perfectly understandable. Think about it. When you walk into an environment, your whole mood can shift depending on the energy present. One of the consequences of this is that you develop an unhealthy desire to want to control every aspect of your personal life. I suffered from terrible obsessive-compulsive disorder for years because of this. I had to turn the lights on and off three times as I entered a room in my house. All the tins in my cupboard had to be facing forward. I had to wash my hands three times every time I touched a doorknob. These are just a few of the outlandish things I would do because I was determined to have control over some aspects of my life.

But the reality is that we have no control over the events that take place in our lives. The economy could crash, and I'd be out of a job. My skills might get taken over by robots, and I'd be out of a job. I can't control how people behave, but I am in full control of my reaction to them. How I react determines the effect that these events have on my life. Accepting you are not in control is difficult, as Murphey's law would have it, the moment you decide to accept that you have no control over the events that take place in your life, a flood of unsettling events are going to show up to test you. You are going to have many challenging setbacks, but if you persevere, you will learn to react in a positive way to every negative circumstance that takes place in your life.

Don't be Consumed by Your Environment: The first time I heard this one, I laughed until I cried. What do you mean? I didn't choose to be an empath. Any environment I walk into consumes me, I can't help it! But what this means is that as soon as you start feeling uncomfortable, instead of embracing the discomfort and absorbing all that negative energy, immediately go into your breathing exercises, visualization, shielding, or whatever method you've chosen to adopt when you are in a situation that makes you feel overwhelmed.

Think Like a Golfer: Contrary to popular belief, Tiger Woods has had more bad shots than good ones. It's all the bad shots that got him prepared for those amazing shots you see him take on the golf course. Golfers don't give up because of all the bad shots, they get really excited when they have that one good shot, and all their energy goes into recreating and improving that shot. That's the same attitude you need to have when things don't go the way you had planned. Don't focus on the fact that it went wrong; focus on the things that went well for you during the day, recreate those moments, and work on improving them.

Focus on the Opportunity and Not the Challenge: There is an opportunity in every challenge if you look for it. Let me tell you a story that my favorite public speaker, Les Brown, told. Two friends had been working for a company for years. When the economy started going bad, the company was forced to let go of some of its employees, and these two friends lost their jobs. The next day they started looking for work. They traveled to and called every company they knew of, but because the country was in a recession, no one was hiring. One friend got depressed and decided to give up. The other friend was determined to look for work, and that is what he did. He kept pounding the pavement and making phone calls. Eventually, he decided to volunteer for a company and work for no pay. The manager agreed, but made sure he was certain that this was an unpaid position. He went to work every single day, he was the first person to show up, and the last person to leave despite the fact that he wasn't getting paid. He did this for a good few months, and his work ethic was greatly admired. One morning, the manager called him into the office and explained that one of the supervisors was leaving and he would like to hire him for the job. Of course, he was delighted and accepted the position without hesitation.

The moral of the story is that the man who ended up with a job focused on the opportunity and not the challenge. He created an opportunity for himself by volunteering and chose not to focus on the challenge of being out of work. His decision paid off.

It's human nature to focus on the problem, but the very nature of the empath is to solve problems. We have a tendency to want to save the world when our internal world is still broken. We brush our problems under the carpet and focus on everyone else's. Now it's time to apply the same approach to your own life.

Start Zoom Focusing: Empaths find it difficult to get things done because they are so consumed with being overwhelmed all the time. I always knew I had a writing gift and that I wanted to write my own books one day. But it took me ten years to write my first book! Why? Because I couldn't focus. Every day, I would tell myself I would either start writing first thing in the morning, or when I came home from work. It never happened; something else was always consuming my mental space. I just couldn't get it together. I always came home and climbed into bed because I was so drained from the day. But I would zap my own energy even further by thinking about the things that took place throughout the day that drained my energy. In the morning, I would work myself up about having to go to work and deal with negative energy. It wasn't until I started implementing the energy protection strategies in Chapter Four that I was able to start getting things done.

Once I developed positive habits, my life changed. On my way home from work, I would play a motivational speech and repeat empath affirmations. By the time I got home, I was charged with positive energy. I would then take an Epsom salt bath, purge myself of the negative energy that had gathered in my palms, have my dinner, and start writing. I wrote my first book within six months.

Additionally, I found it extremely helpful to write out a routine list and a 21-day checklist. I stick them on my wall by my light switch, so I'm forced to look at them every day. Your daily routine list should look something like this:

- 6 am: wake up
- Write in gratitude journal
- Meditate
- Take a shower
- Have breakfast

- Go to work and listen to something motivational on the way

The 21-day checklist is just numbers, 1, 2, 3, 4 … up until 21 that you cross off with a red pen every day you complete your routine. When you fail, you've got to go back to day 1. Once you've completed the 21 days, put up another 21 days.

At the end of that list should be the actions you need to take each day to achieve your goals. Mine was to write a book, and so my one and only zoom focus requirement was to write 200 words a day, and that's exactly what I did until the book was complete. I stopped focusing on the things that didn't serve me and made sure I had completed my action steps before I did anything else. Zoom focusing is a very effective way to get things done. You will be surprised at how much you can accomplish when you cut out the non-essentials.

Get Clear About Your Purpose

Okay, so you know that you're an empath and your gift is not a curse but a major blessing. It shouldn't just be a blessing to you, but to everyone you are divinely connected to. The question now becomes, how are you going to use your gift to make the world a better place? Let's start by defining the word purpose.

What is Purpose? In short, your purpose is the reason why you were created. As far as I'm concerned, human beings were created, and the creator put us on Earth to fulfill a specific purpose. The person who created books created them for people to read. The person who created chairs created them for people to sit on. The person who created airplanes created them for people to fly around the world. There is nothing on Earth that wasn't designed to do something. I want you to stop for a minute and perform a little exercise:

- Pay attention to your surroundings. What is the first thing you notice?
- I notice a yellow highlighter.
- What is that thing used for?
- My highlighter is used to go over text I read that I find interesting.
- How does the thing you've noticed improve your life?
- My highlighter makes it easy for me to find the parts in the text that I found interesting.

Empath Secrets

Why did I make you do this exercise? Because I want you to understand that everything that has been created was done so to solve a problem. The person who created highlighters got fed up with not being able to find important texts. In doing so, he solved this problem for millions of people around the world. The person who created the laptop did so because they were fed up with having to go and look for a computer every time they needed to access the internet when they left their home.

There is a problem on Earth that you were created to fix. It is uniquely tailored to the gifts you've been given, and that extends beyond your empath gift. I've always known I could write, but I didn't know how I could use my gift to solve a problem. It was only when I broke down the meaning of purpose that I discovered what I was created for. I am an empath. I've developed it into a superpower, and now I'm using my writing gift to send a message out into the world to help other empaths who are struggling with their gift. So, how can you develop a sense of purpose?

Read: Reading connects you with people you will probably never meet, or, if you are reading fiction novels, don't exist. You will find that when you read a fiction novel, all the characters are there for a reason, no matter how small or large their role in the story. With non-fiction books like memoirs, the author has found a clear sense of purpose in telling their story. People write memoirs for all sorts of reasons, but one of them is to document their lives in a way that gives others in a similar situation a clear understanding of what they are currently experiencing in life. What I found was that the more I read, the more I focused on my own purpose. I would analyze the lives of the people in the books I was reading and pay attention to how they were contributing to the world around them. Something else I used to do was pay attention to the bad guys. I came to the conclusion that they were using their gifts in reverse. For example, bullies are typically people who have endured trauma in the home. Their response to that abuse is to take out their anger on other people when really their purpose is to heal people from the same trauma they were inflicted with.

If you are experiencing a crisis of purpose, take a trip to your local library and pick out some books that mean something to you, and start reading.

What Other People Appreciate About You: Most of us operate in our purpose without realizing it because that's what comes naturally to us. When I think back, I have always been told how great of a writer I am. Anytime anyone wanted something written, my friends and family would reach out to me. At work, when it came to writing something memorable on a card, I was always asked to do it. While I was doing it, I didn't think about it; the words would flow out of me, I would hand it to the person, and they would gush over how well it was written. I would say thank you, shrug my shoulders, and get on with something else. But through every writing request and every compliment, the powers that be were letting me know that this is what I was born to do. I had thought about finding a career in writing, but every time I looked into it, I got scared. There were too many qualifications to get and too many hoops to jump through to make it in that industry. I kept putting the idea to bed until I was forced to confront it. You will find that the thing you are most scared of doing is the thing you are supposed to do.

Find Your Tribe: When you are surrounded by people who don't appreciate you, it becomes increasingly difficult to find your purpose. Before I stepped into my superpower, not only did I have a narcissistic partner, my friends were also extremely toxic. I would go as far as to say that they were narcissists too. They mocked me for being too sensitive. I was constantly told to "get over it," no one ever listened to me, and the only time they saw me as useful was when they needed something written. My social life was a complete nightmare. But when I left my husband and started therapy, I was introduced to new people through my group therapy classes. Some of them were empaths or highly sensitive people, and we understood each other. There was a compassion and understanding between us that I had never experienced before. It was through this group that I resurrected my writing dream. We had to write something for one of our classes, and everyone was so in awe of what I had written, but it didn't end there. I was told that I should write a book. Something clicked from that moment, and there was a shift within me. They kept encouraging me until the book was written.

Turn Your Pain into Power: I hated my life for many years. I was frustrated, tired, and depressed every day. But once I developed the strength to leave, I became unstoppable. The only way I can describe it is that I had been freed from prison. I was no longer in captivity and bondage to someone who didn't have my best interests at heart. Today, I tell my story with pride, not because I am proud of the fact that I let a man abuse me for so long, but that I found the strength to become all who I knew I was destined to be. I get letters from all over the world from people thanking me for telling my story and how it empowered them to leave an abusive relationship and turn their life around. I now know that my labor wasn't in vain. I didn't go through what I went through for nothing. Thousands of women have taken my burden and turned it into a blessing. I can now thank my husband for the hell that he put me through.

Stop Giving Away Your Power

OH MY GOODNESS! This used to be my favorite pastime; obviously, it wasn't intentional because I didn't know I was doing it, but I was the queen of giving away my power. I could write a book about it. Every time you let someone take you out of character, you are giving away your power. When you allow a person to make you feel bad, think negative thoughts, or behave differently, you have given that individual access to your soul. I'm not talking about subtle changes in behavior that don't have a negative influence on your life. For example, I have a friend who is Christian. She takes her faith very seriously, and she doesn't swear. Now, she doesn't tell me not to swear around her because she knows that not everyone has the same level of self-control as her. She doesn't get in the least bit offended because people swear when they are around her. However, I noticed that she doesn't swear. I mean, I have literally never heard a cuss word come out of her mouth. So when I'm around her, I make a conscious decision not to swear. It's taken several years, but I don't swear anymore because of her. That subtle change in behavior was actually of great benefit to me. What I am talking about is things like allowing people to criticize you in a way that is disrespectful, but you sit there and suck it up because you don't want to come across as rude. Instead of saying what you really want to say, you internalize your anger, which drains your mental energy. It took some practice, but I eventually learned to stop giving away my power, and it has been one of the most liberating things I've ever done. Here's how I did it.

Own Your Emotions: Now, all empaths know that they absorb other people's emotions. That's not what I'm referring to here. I mean your emotions. When you are feeling insecure, guilty, or angry, no one forced you to feel like this. You chose to accept those emotions. The reality is that people can be annoying, and sometimes extremely rude. There is absolutely nothing you can do about this because you have no control over how other people behave. But you do have control over how you react to other people's behavior. When someone is offending you, and you can feel your emotions changing for the worst, you can either walk away or do some of the breathing exercises in Chapter Four to calm you down. If you walk away, engage in positive self-talk to cancel out the negative energy you've been exposed to.

Allow Other People to Own Their Emotions: Taking on other people's emotions is what empaths do best. But it's important to remember that how people feel is not your responsibility; in fact, it has nothing to do with you. It is perfectly okay to express empathy and see things from the other person's point of view, but that's as far as it should go. You can't make someone feel happy, nor can you make someone feel angry about a situation if that's not how they feel.

See Everything as a Choice

Life is about making choices. There are no absolutes. Empaths are notorious for getting their knickers in a twist about every little decision. The reality is that you don't have to go shopping with your sister, nor do you have to turn up at your best friend's cousin's birthday party. Empaths don't like saying no to anything because they don't want to offend anyone. So if you get two invites in a day, let's use the example above. You are going to agree to both of them and then stress yourself out because you've surrendered your entire day to participate in activities that you have zero interest in. When you realize that everything is a choice, you will stop allowing other people to run your life and take full responsibility for it. I have a lot more free time to do the things I love now that my weekends and evenings are not packed with what I've termed, "yes, yes activities." I used to hate my life. I was always bouncing from one place to the next, feeling overwhelmed and anxious because I couldn't bear the thought of saying no. Things really changed for me once I started seeing everything as a choice.

Forgive and Keep it Moving: Forgiveness has nothing to do with the other person and everything to do with you. Marianne Williamson said that unforgiveness is like drinking poison and expecting the other person to die. When someone does something to offend you, trust and do believe that person is not sitting around thinking about you. They couldn't care less; they've gone on with their merry little lives, and you are not even a figment of their imagination. Meanwhile, you are tossing and turning in bed every night angry because of what they did. Get over it! Release the hurt into the sea of forgetfulness and keep it moving.

Forgiveness doesn't mean that you continue a relationship with that person. If it's going to make you feel better to remove them from your life, then do so. But the main point of forgiveness is to release the individual from your spirit, you don't think negative thoughts about them, and neither do you wish them harm. Karma is a very real universal law. Whatever you put out into the world is going to come right back to you. Therefore, there is no point in wishing evil against anyone because, according to universal principles, what you are really doing is wishing the evil on yourself. Additionally, leave the offending party to the will of the universe. Eventually, what they did to you will come right back to them.

Your Self-Worth is Not Based on Someone Else's Opinion: When you allow other people to determine your self-worth, you will never learn to love yourself. What someone else thinks about you has nothing to do with you. This is one of the character traits that keep you on the narcissist's leash. They will love bomb you with compliments and make you feel on top of the world. Then they will tear you down with insults and make you feel like the scum of the earth. This constant roller coaster of compliments and insults gets you hooked. The compliments make you feel so good that you hang on their every last word in the hopes that you will hear them again. In other words, your self-worth is dependent upon how the narcissist views you.

If you want to stop giving away your power, you've got to stop allowing other people to define you. You can do this by becoming the best version of yourself; start working on your goals, go to the gym, volunteer with your favorite organization, become independent, travel. Do the things that make you feel good and refuse to allow anyone to determine your self-worth.

Stop Renting Out Space in Your Brain: How many times have you had an interaction with someone that didn't go too well? Maybe you said the wrong thing, or you struggled to maintain the conversation. You felt so bad about it that you couldn't stop thinking about it; you went to bed thinking about it, you woke up thinking about it, you thought about it on your lunch break, on the way to work. You kept reminding yourself of how embarrassing the situation was and what you could have done instead. This is a complete waste of time. May I remind you that if there is one thing human beings can't do, it's go back in time. You can't go back to the embarrassing moment and redo the situation. Since it's impossible to go back in time, there is no point in thinking about it. The only thing you have control over is how to handle a similar scenario going forward. If you think the interaction didn't go well because you were suffering from social anxiety and were unable to communicate properly, look into taking communication skills classes. Whatever you think you need to do to make your interactions with people better, do it. But one thing you must stop doing is turning over negative situations in your head.

When you catch yourself renting out space in your brain to something that doesn't serve you, kick it out immediately and think about something more pleasing. You may need to take a break and meditate or visualize. Your aim should be to think positive and happy thoughts instead of negative ones.

Stop Complaining: Yep! I said it; stop complaining! Do you want to know why? It's a waste of energy. "Well, how do I stop complaining?" I hear you saying, which is a valid question because it's difficult not to complain. When you work with a ratchet boss and ratchet co-workers, it only makes sense that you call up your girlfriend after work and have a good old moan. But the question you should ask yourself is, what have you accomplished? The answer to this question is absolutely nothing. You spent your 30-minute drive home complaining when you could have spent that time speaking positive affirmations or listening to a motivational speaker. Pay attention to what happens when you complain. You get even more worked up because you begin uncovering more things about the situation or person that aggravated you. Now you are in double overwhelm because of the situation and because you can't stop talking about it and reminding yourself of the situation.

I am in no way suggesting that you don't talk about your problems, because we all need an emotional release. Just make sure when you have a conversation about the offending party, it is constructive and not deconstructive.

Allow Your Values to Guide You: This is another one that I just couldn't get right. The reason why I found it so difficult was because my values changed according to who I was around. I hated offending people, so I would follow their vibe instead of refusing to compromise. When you are clear on your values, you are not going to follow the crowd. Instead, you are going to spend time on the things that are important to you. If you think it's important to work long hours, practice your faith, enjoy your hobbies or value your free time, live this way. Don't allow other people to dictate how you live because you are afraid of what other people think. Additionally, the danger of following the crowd is that when groups of people get together and they have different values, who are you going to follow? You can't follow everyone's values, but you can definitely follow your own.

Takeaways

- You've got to protect your energy at all costs. A strong energy field will ensure that you are capable of operating at your full potential. You can do this by setting boundaries and letting people know that they can't have access to you when they want.

- Your environment should radiate positive energy. You may need to give it a good clean so that negative energy doesn't get trapped and stay in your abode longer than it needs to.
- You can practice yoga, take Epsom salt baths, and meditate to ground and rid yourself of negative energy. Visualization and saying positive affirmations are also great ways to protect your energy.
- You are not alone! You have supernatural assistance available to you through spirit guides and protection angels. You can summon them any time you need help.
- There are a number of things you will need to stop doing to operate in the power that belongs to you. They include eating unhealthy foods and playing the victim.
- Learning how to transmute negative energy is massively important. Not only does it protect you, but you are walking in your purpose by sending positive energy into the universe for those who are ready to receive it.
- There are also several ways you can transmute your own negative energy by applying strategies such as focusing on the opportunities and not the challenges and zoom focusing.

- Getting clear about your purpose is one of the most important things you will do as an empath. When you know why you were put on this earth, it will motivate you to become who you were destined to be.
- Finally, empaths have a bad habit of giving away their power. Once you become conscious that you are doing this, you can apply the required steps to stop.

Conclusion

"The great gift of human beings is that we have the power of empathy." ~ Meryl Streep

Thanks for making it to the end of this book. After reading this, you should have all the information you need to get started in developing your gift. You should be able to understand who you are as an empath. You should be able to determine whether you are a physical, emotional, intuitive, earth, animal, plant, or psychometric empath. You can take the Judith Orloff self-diagnosis test at the end of Chapter One if you are not sure.

I can't emphasize how important it is that you are fully aware of why you believe your empath gift is a curse and not the blessing it was designed to be. I had accepted I was cursed for a long time until I became fully aware of why I thought this way. To free yourself from this bondage, ask yourself the following questions. Does people pleasing leave you exhausted? Do you suffer from depressive episodes? Do you attract toxic people? These are common problems among empaths who are struggling with their gift.

Empath Secrets

Your next step is to understand that change requires work. All the negative experiences you are having as an empath are because you have developed a series of bad habits that cause you to react in a way that is counterproductive to your gift. To get to the next level, you will need to develop good habits to replace the bad ones that are keeping you in bondage.

Protecting your energy as an empath is essential. You can't give everyone access to your soul. It's important that you take the necessary steps to keep yourself free from negative energy. That means you've got to put the appropriate boundaries in place. You will also need to make sure your living environment is conducive to positive energy and that you take part in practices such as yoga and meditation to strengthen your energy field.

Once you've got into the habit of protecting and strengthening your energy, it's time to really dig deep and start practicing the techniques required to take your empath gift to the next level. This includes summoning supernatural help, sharpening your intuition, transmuting negative energy, getting clear on your purpose, and refusing to give away your power.

Before I close, I would like to stress that awakening your superpower is not going to be an easy ride. If you really want to walk in the totality of your power, you will need to put in more effort than the average person. Meditation, visualization, shielding, and everything else that comes with awakening and maintaining your gift takes time and practice. If you are going to get any of these things done before you start your day, you will need to wake up early. I no longer have a 9–5 job, but when I did, I woke up an extra two hours early to complete my daily routine to ensure I was fully grounded before I left the house. When I got back from work, I completed my routine before I engaged in any other activities. Consistency is the key to success in any area of your life. Before I left my husband, I didn't know what consistency was. There was no time to do anything because I was too consumed with being in an abusive relationship. I couldn't even get out of the bed without him giving me permission.

It took me several months to establish a routine, but once I really got consistent and completed my routine for 90 days in a row, the transformation was so dramatic that there was no way I was going back. Without self-discipline, you will never master your gift. "Knowledge is power" is a common phrase, but I would like to change that to "knowledge in action is power." Without applying what you have learned to your life, transformation is impossible. You will remain at first base if you don't put the knowledge you've learned in

Empath Secrets

this book into practice. I can tell you with confidence that it works because I went from zero to hero within six months.

Listen, the world desperately needs you! I once had a bad habit of complaining about how jacked up the world was. I would watch the news, read the papers, listen to the radio, and listen to people and just think there's no hope. I was depressed for a lot of reasons, but one of them was that I felt so sad for the planet. Our creator has given us this amazing universe, and mankind is destroying it. I felt hopeless. It wasn't until I started regaining some strength and understanding my purpose that I realized not only is it my responsibility to change the world, but I have the power to do so.

A part of awakening your superpower is starting with what you've got. Another reason why I was so depressed about the state of the world was because I wanted to be the savior of the world, and I knew that wasn't possible. The reality is that there are some people who don't want help. They are content to remain in their negative energy field, and they don't want to get out. In other words, you couldn't save everyone even if you had the power to do so because some people you would try and help would reject it. You read in Chapter Four that when I set my intention for positive energy to go back into the universe, it should attach itself to someone who is ready and willing to receive it. As much as I would love to save the world, it just isn't possible. So I focus on doing the best I can with the people (like yourself) who are ready to become all who they were created to be for the betterment of humanity.

With that being said, it's time to go. Remember, don't overwhelm yourself with trying to do too much. Start small and work your way up.

I wish you every success on your journey to awakening your superpower and becoming an empowered empath!

Empath Secrets

Thank you!

Before you go, I just wanted to say thank you for purchasing my book. I poured a ton of time into this book and shared a lot of my personal experiences and those of people I spoke to when compiling the book to show you that you're not alone in this, and a beautiful and fulfilling life where you can feel safe and free from abuse is within your grasp.

You just need to reach out and make it happen. Every journey, even one along the road to recovery, starts with a single step. This is your permission to take yours.

It's also a fantastic thought to me that you could have picked from dozens of other books on the same topic, but you took a chance and chose this one.

So, a HUGE thanks to you for getting this book and for reading all the way to the end.

Now I wanted to ask you for a small favor. Could you please consider posting a review on the platform? Your reviews are one of the easiest ways to support the work of independent authors, and it's incredible to go online and see all the amazing support this work has received. I love hearing from you, and hearing your feedback inspires me to write more in the future and helps me to identify what to do better and how to be the best writer I can.

This feedback will help me continue to write the type of books that will help you get the results you want. So if you enjoyed it, please let me know! (-:

Also by Amy White

Digital Minimalism in Everyday Life: Overcome Technology Addiction, Declutter Your Mind, and Reclaim Your Freedom

How to Declutter Your Mind: Secrets to Stop Overthinking, Relieve Anxiety, and Achieve Calmness and Inner Peace

Beginning Zen Buddhism: Timeless Teachings to Master Your Emotions, Reduce Stress and Anxiety, and Achieve Inner Peace

Gaslighting Recovery Workbook: How to Recognize Manipulation, Overcome Narcissistic Abuse, Let Go, and Heal from Toxic Relationships

Resources

Houlihan, B. & Editors of Phoenix International Publications. (2019). *Marvel Super Heroes Spider-man, Avengers, Guardians, and More! - Me Reader Electronic Reader with 8 Book Library - PI Kids* (Second ed.). Phoenix International Publications, Inc.

Lacobani, M. (2008). *Mirroring people: the science of empathy and how we connect with others.* New York: Farrar, Straus, and Giroux.

McLaren, K. (2013). *The Art of Empathy: A Complete Guide to Life's Most Essential Skill* (10/16/13 ed.). Sounds True.

Websites

Bates, S. M. (2014, October 31). *How to Undo Negative Muscle Memory.* Hello Giggles.
https://hellogiggles.com/lifestyle/negative-mental-muscle-memory/

Cristiano Ronaldo. (2014, April 2). The Biography.
https://www.biography.com/athlete/cristiano-ronaldo#:~:text=Early%20Life,of%20his%20father's%20favorite%20actors.

Dunn et al, B. (2010, November 24). *Listening to Your Heart: How Interoception Shapes Emotion Experience and Intuitive Decision Making*. Sage Journals. https://journals.sagepub.com/doi/abs/10.1177/0956797610389191

Edinger, S. (2011, April 11). *Competent Individuals at Risk of Social Undermining*. HR Zone. https://www.hrzone.com/lead/culture/competent-individuals-at-risk-from-social-undermining

Elliot, B. (2018, December 13). *Epson Salt: Benefits Uses and Side Effects*. Healthline. https://www.healthline.com/nutrition/epsom-salt-benefits-uses

Leonard, J. (2018, July 17). *How to Cope With a Depressive Episode*. Medical News Today. https://www.medicalnewstoday.com/articles/322495

Lufityanto et al, G. (2016, April 6). *Measuring Intuition: Nonconscious Emotional Information Boosts Decision Accuracy and Confidence*. Sage Journals. https://journals.sagepub.com/doi/abs/10.1177/0956797616629403

Raypole, C. (2019, December 4). *How to Stop People Pleasing and Still be Nice*. Healthline. https://www.healthline.com/health/people-pleaser

Empath Secrets

Riess, H. (2017, May 9). *The Science of Empathy*. Sage Journals. https://journals.sagepub.com/doi/full/10.1177/2374373517699267

Usher, M. (2011, January 30). *The Impact of the Mode of Thought in Complex Decisions: Intuitive Decisions are Better*. NCBI. https://www.ncbi.nlm.nih.gov/pmc/articles/PMC3110939/

Empathy Definition. (n.d.). Greatergood.Berkeley. Retrieved 21 January 2022, from https://greatergood.berkeley.edu/topic/empathy/definition

What is an Empath. (2019, November 24). Healthlinehttps://www.healthline.com/health/what-is-an-empath

Go With Your Gut - Intuition is More Than a Hunch. (2008, March 5). Leeds University. https://www.leeds.ac.uk/news/article/367/go_with_your_gut__intuition_is_more_than_just_a_hunch_says_leeds_research

The Lizard Man of Matabo. (n.d.). UK Psychics. http://www.ukpsychics.com/lizardman.html

St. Francis of Assisi. (n.d.). Humane Society of America. Retrieved 2 January 2021, from https://www.humanesociety.org/resources/st-francis-assisi

Printed in Great Britain
by Amazon